W9-CMJ-240

AROUND PROUST

AROUND PROUST

RICHARD E. GOODKIN

PRINCETON UNIVERSITY PRESS

PRINCETON, NEW JERSEY

Copyright © 1991 by Princeton University Press
Published by Princeton University Press, 41 William Street,
Princeton, New Jersey 08540
In the United Kingdom: Princeton University Press, Oxford
All Rights Reserved

Library of Congress Cataloging-in-Publication Data

Goodkin, Richard E.
Around Proust / Richard E. Goodkin
p. cm.
Includes bibliographical references and index
ISBN 0-691-06894-1 (cl)—ISBN 0-691-01508-2 (pb)
1. Proust, Marcel, 1871–1922. A la recherche du temps perdu.
2. Proust, Marcel, 1871–1922—Knowledge and learning. I. Title.

PQ2631.R63A7928   1991
843'.912—dc20   90-25443   CIP

This book has been composed in Adobe Palatino

Princeton University Press books are printed on acid-free paper,
and meet the guidelines for permanence and durability of
the Committee on Production Guidelines for Book Longevity of the
Council on Library Resources

Printed in the United States of America by
Princeton University Press,
Princeton, New Jersey

10 9 8 7 6 5 4 3 2 1

10 9 8 7 6 5 4 3 2 1
(Pbk.)

For Charlie Gillespie
1958–1991

IN LOVING MEMORY

CONTENTS

ACKNOWLEDGMENTS

THIS BOOK was completed during the course of a Yale University Senior Faculty Fellowship that I held in 1988–1989: my thanks to the French Department at Yale for their support. I would also like to thank the Department of French and Italian at the University of Wisconsin–Madison, where I was a Visiting Fellow during 1988–1989 and of which I am currently a member, for their generous support.

A shorter version of Chapter 1, "Proust and Home(r): An Avuncular Intertext," was first given as a talk at Mount Holyoke College in November 1987. It was also given in a different form at the International Conference on Narrative Literature at the University of Wisconsin–Madison in April 1989, and appeared in the Comparative Literature issue of *MLN* 104 (1989). Thanks to David Ellison of Mount Holyoke College and William Berg of the University of Wisconsin–Madison for their useful comments and questions. I would also like to thank David Ellison for his openminded and careful reading of the entire manuscript and for his invaluable suggestions. Chapter 2, "T(r)yptext: Proust, Mallarmé, Racine," appeared in *Yale French Studies* 76 (1989); thanks go to Karen Erickson of Saint John's University for several useful suggestions. Chapter 4, "Fiction and Film: Proust's Vertigo and Hitchcock's *Vertigo*," was first given as a talk at the 1985 MLA convention, and a shorter version of the chapter appeared in the Comparative Literature issue of *MLN* 102 (1987). My thanks to Mirella Affron of the College of Staten Island for her helpful comments. A preliminary version of Chapter 5 was given at the MLA convention in 1987 as part of a panel on Proust, and was published under the title "The Proustian Octave: Or, The Scale of Love (and Death)" in *Style* 22, no. 3 (Fall 1988), a special issue devoted to Proust. Thanks to John Halperin of Vanderbilt University, the chair of the panel, to Margaret Miner of Vanderbilt University for first mentioning the Tristan Chord to me in our discussions about Baudelaire and Wagner, and to Jon Bailey of Pomona College for helping me to understand some of the theoretical implications of the Tristan Chord. I am also grateful to Lauren Oppenheim of Princeton University Press for her invaluable comments and criticisms about this chapter.

Thanks are also due various teachers, friends, and students. I think in particular of Robert Roza of Swarthmore College, for the many hours he spent with me discussing my senior thesis on Proust in 1974–1975; of Annette Becker and Jean and Françoise Rueff, for helping to keep me up-to-date on public discussion of Proust in France; and of Claudia Brodsky, for her endless encouragement and wise advice. Among the dozens of students at Yale, both graduate and undergraduate, who have made teaching Proust a great pleasure and who have helped me to approach the novels from many different perspectives, several names come to mind: Myriam Boucharenc, Sarah Winter, Linda Jones, Carole Harris, Margaret Gray-McDonald, Juliann Garey, Margaret Perrow, Valerie Norton, Margit Dementi, Katherine Bonamo, and Vilashini Cooppan.

I would like to thank my family: my mother, Louise, Ira, Marie, Joseph, Kathleen, Mandel, and Roger. Without their support, patience, and love, I would never have written this book.

Finally, I would like to dedicate *Around Proust* to the memory of my partner and companion, Charlie Gillespie. His love, his courage, and his joy in living have been an endless source of inspiration to me.

AROUND PROUST

INTRODUCTION

> To be with someone you love and to think of something
> else: that is how I have my best thoughts, how I best
> discover what is necessary for my work. It is the same
> thing with the text: it produces in me the best sort of
> pleasure if it manages to make itself heard indirectly;
> if, in reading it, I am often led to lift my eyes from
> the page, to hear something else.
> Roland Barthes, *Le Plaisir du texte*

B ECAUSE THE TITLE of this book is meant to be evocative rather
than explanatory, I will begin by speaking about my main goals
in the present study. What I have placed "around Proust" is a
wide variety of things: other literary texts, other (nonliterary) artistic
forms, and other (nonartistic) modes of intellectual pursuit. Certainly
the openness of Proust's monumental cycle of novels, *A la recherche du
temps perdu*, to domains far more numerous than those included in this
book has already been amply demonstrated. What I would like to do
here is to use a number of these recognized connections as the starting
points for a series of readings of Proust's masterpiece.

The artistic and intellectual entities I have chosen to consider in relation to Proust's cycle of novels are extremely diverse in a number of
ways: chronologically, culturally, aesthetically, and epistemologically.
They come from periods ranging from antiquity (Homer, Zeno of Elea)
to the 1950s (Hitchcock). They belong to the cultures of the Greek,
French, German, and English-speaking worlds. And they take such diverse forms as epic, lyric poetry, film, and psychological treatise. And
yet in spite of their variety of medium and perspective, my premise is
that at some level all of these works and theories interact with Proust's
text in similar ways; their interaction can show us something complex
and thought-provoking about both Proust's novel and the artistic and
nonartistic forms being placed alongside it.

I hope that the analyses that follow, each of which places a work or
a theory in tandem with Proust's novel, will show that Proust's text—in
spite of its much-commented-upon length and the impression it gives
of having exhausted every topic about which it speaks (not to mention
the reader)—comes into its own when it is drawn out of itself. Perhaps
a useful way to speak about Proust, then, is to speak "around" Proust,
in conjunction with a series of literary, artistic, and intellectual "oth-

ers." Proust's work most becomes itself when it is seen indirectly, "around" others.

Readers of Proust may well wonder about the value of adding anything to the three-thousand-page (or, in the new Pléiade edition with its seemingly endless *brouillons*, four-thousand-page) cycle of novels. It is inevitable that any critical or analytical approach to a text must bring to it elements that come from outside of the text itself, but a reader struck by the unsurpassed consistency of Proust's cycle might begin to feel that if there is a work of literature that stands on its own, this is it.

A la recherche du temps perdu certainly belongs to the category of masterpieces that give the impression of being utterly self-contained, of creating a universe that, although infinitely complex, retains tremendous internal coherence. This is true whether one examines the work's largest issues or its most minute details, the role of involuntary memory or that of Théodore, the grocery boy at Combray. As the French would say, *tout se tient*: it all holds together. Proust even had the consideration to incorporate into his novel a discussion of what the narrator's ideal novel would be like. And whether *A la recherche du temps perdu* is or is not intended to be that novel,[1] many critics have applied this self-proclaimed *ars poetica*, taken from the last volume of the cycle, to the work itself and found it to be the crowning element of the cycle's internal coherence—whence, perhaps, the tendency of critical works about Proust to pastiche his style, to paraphrase the analyses he himself provides in the novel, and to mimic his title. The effect of all this is to emphasize still further the novel's consistency.

This consistency, however, can be viewed from quite a different perspective; approached with even the slightest irreverence, the novel actually encourages us to do so. The consistency of the novel can be taken as a function of its obsessiveness, of its narrator's inability ever to break out of himself. Like the young Marcel so intent on his good-night kiss that he appears on the verge of imploding, the novel has a strong, almost irresistible centripetal force that draws all concerns toward itself and expresses them in its own terms. And although the novel tells us again and again that obsessiveness is the human condition, it also reminds us of the limiting nature of obsession.

It is perhaps for this reason that the novel also repeatedly attempts to reach outside of itself, and this in part accounts for its astonishing breadth. This is a work whose uniformity is matched only by its scope; a work that devotes what appears to be equal care and attention to a dizzying array of questions large and small, from the nature of love to the Duchesse de Guermantes's motives for pulling in her shoulders as she enters a room; from the function and limits of memory to the functioning of Charles Swann's bladder. One feels that everything in the work holds together, certainly—but one also comes to sense that much of everything in the world somehow finds its way into the work in one form or another. What we are confronted with, then, is a text that faces both inward and outward; that is built around a phenomenal consistency but also invites us to resist its inwardness; that gives an unremitting uniformity to everything within its enormous confines, and yet constantly reaches out to make new and unexpected connections.

Indeed, Proust's gargantuan digressions—lengthy parenthetical inserts, labyrinthine subordinate clauses, indefinitely prolonged appositions, and pages spent on asides of extraordinary complexity—contribute to this sense that the text, in spite of its singlemindedness, is never satisfied with the range of topics about which it purportedly speaks. And, in fact, another of my goals in speaking "around" Proust—that is, in speaking about Proust by seeming to speak about other things—is to recognize the importance of digression to his literary enterprise.

Digression—speaking *around* the point rather than *to* the point—may seem a peculiar basis for a work, whether a work of fiction, like Proust's *A la recherche du temps perdu*, or a work about such a work, like this one. But the fact that Proust is, among other things, a master of digression is apparent in the very conception and development of his novel. As has been demonstrated by a number of *études de genèse*, Proust first envisioned only three novels, the substance of which more or less corresponded to just the beginning and the end of the cycle as we now have it. When its full publication was delayed by the First World War, the work began to grow—but it did not grow by extending beyond the end; rather, it grew from the middle. As Antoine Compagnon puts it:

> "Combray" and the "Matinée at the Princesse de Guermantes's" [the first and last sections of the prewar project] thus define the two extreme supports of a prodigious stetched bow. They are so powerfully constructed, so necessary to each other in their interdependence, that between them the novel was subsequently able to stretch out as much as it pleased and to take in numerous unexpected developments—sometimes even causing a certain amount of interference—without losing its form or momentum. It is as if the beginning and the end held the cycle of novels so tightly together that nearly anything could fit into the middle.[2]

If the conclusion, the grand scene of revelation in which the narrator finally comes to realize the ultimate, overriding value of the work of art, is the novel's goal, then practically all Proust did between 1913 (when *Du côté de chez Swann* was published) and 1922 (the year of his death) was to make it more difficult for the reader—and for Proust himself—to reach that goal. One could interpret this function of indefinitely expandable digression in any number of ways, whether abstract

and theoretical—resistance to closure—or concrete and thematic—the
furtive expansion of the homosexual motif in the fleshing-out of the
characters of Albertine, Charlus, and Morel. But recent Proust criticism
has begun to focus attention on the fact that one effect of this seemingly
boundless burgeoning-out[3] of Proust's novel is a questioning—perhaps even an undermining—of the very conclusions that Proust's rampant digressions postpone.

Proust's novel can of course be read—and indeed was generally read
for at least a half-century—as a lengthy expansion of the initial episode
of the madeleine that is at the same time a gradual preparation for the
final epiphany that comes in *Le Temps retrouvé*, an epiphany that brings
a final sense of order to the novel. But it can also be read, and is beginning to be read, as an unwieldy, unruly, and in some respects unquan-
tifiable piece of fiction that is actually not very well suited to—or, at the
very least, not satisfactorily accounted for by—its much-touted conclusion. As Compagnon puts it:

> Proust absolutely wants to reach certain laws, but his book nonetheless con-
> tradicts their very hypothesis. True intermittences, those of the heart and
> those of art, do not fall under the authority of any law, unlike reminiscences,
> which are in themselves reducible to a theory of memory. Thus any reading
> of the *Recherche* that seeks to pin the novel down to the reference and theories
> that Proust uses to justify it is deceptive: the novel heads off in a different
> direction, and the critical gap between what it says it does and what it actu-
> ally does is much more important.[4]

The direction in which the novel heads off is not the end of the novel as
it is presented to us. This is a novel that, in a fundamental sense, does
not progress toward its own conclusion. The novel's conclusion is a
kind of literary *trompe-l'oeil*, a somewhat simplistic, two-dimensional
treatise passing for something profound. Like an actual, physical
trompe-l'oeil, when perceived from far away—as the distant goal toward which the rest of the cycle leads—it appears to have depth, but if
one examines it closely rather than simply accepting its claims to be the
crowning achievement of the cycle, it turns out to be quite flat. At the
very least it is far less interesting than the path leading up to it.[5]

Thus the novel's "true" direction is the direction it took when it became a novel of endless digression, when it lost its way and started to
indulge in lengthy developments with only a tenuous link to what the
novel purports to be about, to tell what Max Unold admiringly calls
"pointless stories" that gradually become fascinating and irresistible.[6]
As Paul Valéry elegantly puts it in speaking about the tangential style
of Proust's novel, "all [its] divergences [*écarts*] belong to [it]."[7] In the
past quarter-century it has become a critical cliché to begin the titles of
books and articles with the preposition "toward," an impulse that un-

doubtedly stems from a laudable sense of humility: to move "toward" a particular area of inquiry is to recognize that one will never reach the final goal of finding answers to all one's questions. If we accept the idea that the conclusion of Proust's novel does not in fact answer all the questions raised by the narrator's search—and even that his goal is in a sense an illusory one—it might seem appropriate to entitle this book *Toward Proust*.

But once we have accepted the primacy of digression in the novel, once we have understood that digression comes to take on a value in itself, can we not take the idea of "toward . . ." one step further by emphasizing the detours one can take if one relinquishes the idea that reaching a goal is of the utmost importance? This does not mean that these readings of Proust's novel purport to be devoid of a goal. Rather, what I have attempted to borrow from Proust—for in the end no work on Proust is entirely free of the mimetic fallacy, the often subconscious urge to imitate one's author—is the notion that the path is more important than the destination. It is my hope that the conclusions of these readings will in fact ring true, but for me an equally compelling goal is to form what leads up to them, the groundwork of the analyses, into a thought-provoking network of interpretation.

. . . . .

The two principal components of reading "around" Proust—grouping other works and perspectives around Proust's text and recognizing the primacy of digression in the novel—are both closely related to the critical practice of intertextuality, which is important, whether implicitly or explicitly, to all the analyses that follow. While one can, theoretically, speak of intertextual links among the works of a single author, or even among different sections of a single work, most intertextual analyses are based on some kind of grouping of works by different authors. The grouping may be based on an explicit allusion of one work to another; it may be the product of the critic's imagination, in which case he or she must justify juxtaposing the texts in question; or the critic may start with the idea that a given text contains a covert, often subconscious allusion to another text, in which case that shadowy interplay of texts must be brought into the light of day.

Any of these strategies for grouping texts together may lead to a valuable intertextual reading; in fact there need be no essential difference among readings using these various starting points. The question of whether an author is conscious of alluding to another text—or even, to sidestep the thorny issue of authorial intention, whether a *text* is conscious of interacting with another text—is to my mind not an especially interesting question, for the answer is always both yes and no. To the extent that a literary text belongs to a broadly defined cultural tradition that creates—indeed, that is largely composed of—a potentially infinite number of relations between different artistic and intellectual works spanning many centuries, a given work may be said to interact with other works—to speak in a similar or dissenting voice, to use analogous terms, to come to the same or opposite conclusions, and so on— whether or not its author was familiar with those other works. On the other hand, even when authors are familiar with other works, and even when they are aware of alluding to them in some way, they are certainly no more conscious of all the different ways in which their text might be said to interact with those other works than they are of all the possible interpretations of their own work.

The groupings that form the bases for this series of readings are thus quite varied in nature. In some instances—and specifically in Chapter 1, Chapter 2, and Chapter 5—I have dealt with connections that the novel openly establishes. In the first two chapters I have worked from literary allusions within Proust's text: to the *Odyssey* in Chapter 1, and to several works of Mallarmé and Racine in Chapter 2. Along the same lines, Chapter 5 elaborates upon connections between Proust's work and the Tristan Chord of Wagner's *Tristan and Isolde*. Even in these instances of starting from the novel's overt reference to other works, however, I have been conscious of having to justify by the analyses themselves the lengthy development of what might at first seem to be essentially parenthetical allusions in Proust's text.

In the other three chapters, Chapters 3, 4, and 6, I have developed relations that the text itself does not make explicit. Chapter 3 deals with the novel's affinity with the pre-Socratic philosopher Zeno, through the mediation of Proust's contemporary, Henri Bergson; Chapter 4 considers the novel as an anticipation of the cinematic future and analyzes the Hitchcock film *Vertigo* as an anomalous version of it; and Chapter 6 examines the relations between Proust's depiction of mourning and that of Sigmund Freud. In each of these cases I have made links that the novel does not make. I cannot be certain that Proust read the pre-Socratics at all, let alone in any depth, even if Bergson certainly did. It is unlikely that Proust was familiar with the specifics of Freud's theory of mourning, the central text of which appeared while Proust was working frenetically on his novel. And we can be quite sure that Proust never had the pleasure of viewing Alfred Hitchcock's film *Vertigo*, which was first screened nearly forty years after Proust's death (although it is quite possible, as we shall see, that Hitchcock was familiar with Proust). Moreover, in none of these cases does the work or theory by way of which I read Proust's text share with it any direct link through tradition. None of these other works are novels, none of them are French, and only one of them is roughly contemporary with the composition of Proust's novel.

Associating Proust's text with these seemingly unrelated works and theories might seem to undermine the very conception of a readily identifiable tradition that provides the implicit underpinning for many (if not most) intertextual readings. But I want to emphasize the double value of tradition here and the implications of that double value for the practice of intertextuality. A literary tradition can be perceived as essentially exclusive or essentially inclusive. It can be thought to establish fixed criteria that both determine which works are a part of it and define set relations between those works, or to form a flexible network that provides an ongoing means of both integrating works into itself and making new connections between works. Because of the link between tradition and canonization that has been made in recent criticism, tradition has come to be perceived as a form of exclusion or repression as often as a form of inclusion or incorporation. As has been clearly demonstrated, tradition can be a form of political and social tyranny, and can be used to exclude people on the basis of gender, race, and social class, among other factors.

I would like to suggest that tradition and canonization implicitly play a role in the practice of intertextuality as well, and that here, too, tradition is bivalent; it can be a form of tyranny or a form of empowerment. A great many of the links established by criticism that calls itself intertextual are actually quite conventional, limited to works of the same period, language, genre, or all three. But a critic can also fruitfully juxtapose works that do not obviously belong to the same tradition (the delineation of a given tradition being a particularly complex and unstable issue), and in that case one might say that it is the critic who is trying to create (or perhaps extend) tradition by revealing the unexpected ways in which seemingly unrelated works can be connected. The readings of Proust's text presented here, all of which are based on points of contact with other works, are in no way intended to be definitive or exhaustive discussions. Rather, it is my hope that they will contribute to the infinite network of relations and correspondences linking various artistic and intellectual pursuits, a network that itself can be said to "make up" a tradition in the double sense of the term: to constitute and to invent.

In this sense Proust's text enters into an exchange with all the works and theories examined here. It changes them and is changed by them, and I believe this sort of exchange—which need not be strictly limited by temporal, national, or generic boundaries—both depends upon and demonstrates the potential openness of literary tradition (and of intertextuality). It is of precisely this kind of openness that T. S. Eliot speaks when in "Tradition and the Individual Talent" he discusses the impossibility of establishing closure in literary tradition:

> What happens when a new work of art is created is something that happens simultaneously to all the works of art which preceded it. The existing monuments form an ideal order among themselves, which is modified by the introduction of the new (the really new) work of art among them. The existing order is complete before the new work arrives; for order to persist after the supervention of novelty, the *whole* existing order must be, if ever so slightly, altered; and so the relations, proportions, values of each work of art toward the whole are readjusted.... Whoever has approved this idea of order ... will not find it preposterous that the past should be altered by the present as much as the present is directed by the past.[8]

In a very different spirit, Roland Barthes, speaking of Proustian intertextuality, comes to a surprisingly similar conclusion: "I relish ... the reversal of origins, the flexibility which makes the earlier text come from the later text."[9]

Seen in this light, tradition does not designate a group of works that inevitably belong together for reasons of form, theme, style, genre, convention, and authorial intention. It is neither a constraint that dictates what kinds of works we should or should not read together, nor an authority that justifies our making certain sorts of connections without further ado—and at times, consequently, without much concern for acknowledging the complexity of the works in question. Rather, tradition can be an effort to build bridges in unexpected places, to explore the kinds of relations that can be established by any reader, the only necessary (and indeed sufficient) justification for which is the subtlety of the reading offered.

Discovering indirect relations among works often involves paying particularly close attention to what might seem like unimportant details, for as Walter Benjamin points out in a remarkable essay on Proust, "we do not always proclaim loudly the most important thing we have to say."[10] And it is here, in fact, that we return to digression, the second element that defines reading "around" Proust and one that also more generally characterizes the nature of the intertextual readings I propose here. Proust's text, perhaps more than any other text, rewards what one might call "digressive" reading—reading for details, searching for the unexpected, seeking out the ways in which a text is often most interesting when it is caught off guard. Intertextuality itself is a kind of digression, since one of its premises is that a given text actually speaks about something other than itself and must be read with other texts in mind. Thus the intertextual readings I offer here might themselves be considered digressive insofar as they take Proustian digression as a principle of reading. My analyses will not necessarily highlight the most famous and conspicuous passages of the *Recherche*—although I will certainly have occasion to mention the madeleine scene, the good-night kiss, and the scene in the Guermantes' library in *Le Temps retrouvé*, for example—but will often focus, rather, on passages that would not generally find their way into either a résumé of the work or a list of its most significant scenes.

In addition to reading digressively and thus developing intertexts that might themselves be called digressive, another goal I have pursued in this book is to broaden the domain of intertextuality beyond the limits of the strictly textual—that is, beyond readings that link two literary texts. Strictly speaking, only the first section of the book belongs to the realm of intertextuality; only this section deals with the relations between Proust's text and other literary texts. But, in dealing both with other artistic media (cinema in Chapter 4, music in Chapter 5) and with nonartistic modes of thought and expression (philosophy in Chapter 3, psychology in Chapter 6), I believe that my analyses remain intertextual in some sense. By moving beyond the provinces of literature and textuality, the interaction between Proust's text on the one hand and nonliterary texts and other artistic forms on the other can teach us something about literary textuality. It is difficult to speak of Hitchcock's or Wagner's "texts," but the kinds of relations I am trying to establish between Proust's text and these works of art highlight certain characteristics—and, indeed, certain limits—of Proustian textuality. In anticipating the cinematic future of Hitchcock's *Vertigo* or recalling Wagner's *Tristan and Isolde*, Proust's novel defines its own literariness and textuality in a way that is perhaps more striking than in the novel's interactions with other literary texts. Similarly, although Proust's novel is neither a work of applied philosophy nor a work of applied psychology, examining the novel from the perspective of certain philosophical and psychological issues can help to indicate how receptive Proust's text is to these two domains of intellectual endeavor, as well as how it ultimately distinguishes itself from them. The novel approaches philosophical and psychological problems, just as it approaches cinematic and musical genres, in an eminently literary way.

Those chapters that are not strictly literary may require a particular open-mindedness of the reader. Although probably no one would deny the fact that Proust was interested in Wagner, perhaps not everyone will accept the suggestion that Proust attempts, perhaps subconsciously, to appropriate certain features of musicality through correspondences among letters and pitch names and scales. Along the same lines, it is clear—and, given the form of his novel, easy to understand—that Proust had serious objections to cinema on aesthetic grounds, so that it may take a good deal of convincing to demonstrate that his novel can be said at times to look toward cinema as a potential means of escape (albeit an ambivalent one) from the constraints of fiction.

In addition to moving from strictly literary discussions in Part I to analyses linking Proust's work with nonliterary and nonartistic domains in Parts II and III, I have divided the book into three sections of two chapters each, in order to give the reader an impression of returning to a single issue or question from different perspectives—something that the novel itself does repeatedly. The ubiquitous feeling of *déjà vu* in Proust has as a corollary that of *jamais vu la première fois*. To return to any passage after completing the entire cycle is to return to a different passage than one read the first time. This is not to say that the second time is any more valid or "correct" than the first time was: as we shall see in Chapter 5, the recurrent motif of retrospective understanding in Proust is something of a red herring. What it does mean, rather, is that the novel emphasizes again and again the limitations of any single perspective. Thus Part I, "Proust and Intertextuality," examines the relations among Proust's work and several different literary genres (epic in Chapter 1, lyric and tragedy in Chapter 2). Parts II and III each deal with a central issue in Proust's work as seen from two very different perspectives. Part II, "Representation of Time and Movement," discusses the incommensurability of the temporal, first from the perspective of philosophy and then from that of cinema. Part III, "Love and Death," examines the ways in which Proust's text uses the articulation between these two motifs, first from a musical point of view and then from a psychological perspective.

Like the juxtapositions of Proust's work with others that form the basis for this book, the relations between the chapters in each section are meant to have a certain coherence and yet remain flexible. Part I deals strictly with literary works, albeit works belonging to different centuries and linguistic traditions. Part III looks at works belonging to a single language (German) and to the same general period, but the works in question are radically different in form. And Part II discusses works of two creative thinkers (Zeno and Hitchcock) that share neither the same language nor the same medium—nor even the same millenium.

The apparent differences separating the works grouped in a single section may in fact belie similarities in the analyses of the works, and vice versa. The works of Zeno and Hitchcock seem to have very little in common, but their interactions with Proust's text raise remarkably similar issues relating to the impossibility of measuring and representing time and movement adequately. Conversely, while it would be fairly easy to place Wagner and Freud within a shared cultural context—one can easily imagine teaching their works within the framework of a single course, for example—the conclusions I have reached in Chapters 5 and 6 may almost seem to be mutually exclusive, or at least in conflict with one another. In particular, these two chapters present contrasting views of love: in Chapter 5 the obstacles to love are seen as a source of deepening, as what gives strength to the grandmother's final expression of love in death, an expression that, as we shall see, is fundamentally musical. In Chapter 6, by contrast, the grandmother's resistance to love, which increasingly dominates her personality, is not resolved by her death but rather is simply passed on to Marcel, and ultimately becomes incorporated into the narrator's perspective. The differences in these two readings are as much a function of the difference in perspective of the two analyses—one musical, one psychological—as they are a function of Proust's text itself.

The young Marcel believes that every member of an audience viewing a dramatic production in a theater sees a set that is built just for his or her own eyes, and in *Le Temps retrouvé* we are told that "Every reader is, when he reads, the reader of himself." Let us extend these Proustian truisms to other domains and hope that reading Proust's novel through the perspective of other literary and nonliterary texts and other artistic modes can teach us something not only about the novel itself, but also about other intellectual forms of expression.

PART I

PROUST AND INTERTEXTUALITY

Chapter 1

PROUST AND HOME(R):

AN AVUNCULAR INTERTEXT

THE AVUNCULAR LIE

I F, AS PETER BROOKS points out, "paternity is a dominant issue within the great tradition of the nineteenth-century novel,"[1] perhaps it is not surprising that Proust, that perennial "perverter"[2] of time and other things, would transform the issue of paternity into an issue of avuncularity.[3] In Proust the paternal relation that dominates the nineteenth-century novel[4] is not so much replaced as *dis*placed: to the vertical axis of family structure, which marks the movement between the generations, is added the horizontal, or fraternal/sororal, axis, which deals with what Edward Said calls relations of "adjacency" rather than origin,[5] and the combination of these two axes, parental and sibling, gives us the avuncular relation. In this chapter I examine the relation between Proust's novel and the *Odyssey* by way of a series of Homeric allusions that Proust makes, and I define that relation in terms of what I would like to call "avuncular" intertextuality. If the study of literary sources can be said to be a sort of "parental" enterprise, one of my premises here is that intertextuality is not a relation between a "parent" text and its offspring, but rather a relation that, while it may start out trying to provide a simple link between two generations, is always sidetracked or "avuncularized."

The relations between Proust's novel and the *Odyssey* in fact center around the issue of avuncularity, and this is already true in the first of the five passages of Proust's novel that refer to the *Odyssey*. This occurs in Balbec, when Marcel and Saint-Loup are invited to dine at the house of Bloch, Marcel's school friend. There we meet M. Nissim Bernard, Bloch's great-uncle, or, more precisely, "l'oncle à héritage de Mme Bloch"[6]—that is, Bloch's mother's rich uncle, who will leave his money to the Bloch family. Uncle Nissim tells a highly improbable tale: he says that he knows Saint-Loup's father, the Marquis de Marsantes. Of course nobody believes that Nissim Bernard, a Jew without any obvious social connections, might know the aristocratic Marquis. Moreover, Nissim Bernard is known to be a pathological liar, and it is as a liar that he is compared to Odysseus:

The uncle told his acquaintances in the hotel . . . that he was a senator. Even though he could be sure that one day they would find out the title was false, he still couldn't resist the need to appropriate it at the time. M. Bloch suffered a great deal from his uncle's lies and all the problems they caused. "Don't pay any attention to him, he's a real kidder," he said quietly to Saint-Loup. . . . "Even more of a liar than Ithakan Odysseus, whom Athena called the biggest liar in the world," our friend Bloch added. "Well what do you know!" cried out M. Nissim Bernard, "I sure didn't expect to have dinner with my friend's son! But in Paris I have your father's photo and loads of letters from him. He always used to call me 'Uncle,' no one knows why." (1.775)

Uncle Nissim is given two salient attributes in this, his first appearance in the novel: he is a liar, and he is an uncle—doubly an uncle, in fact, since not only is he Bloch's real uncle but he also becomes, in his tale about Saint-Loup's father, the latter's substitute uncle. But why, we might ask, should an uncle be a pathological liar—or, more precisely, why should a pathological liar be an uncle? In order to answer this question, we must digress long enough to do a preliminary examination of the nature of family relations in our two works.

Narrative Axes and Family Axes

I would like to approach this question of the avuncular lie by way of a parallel between family structures and narrative structures in both Proust's and Homer's works.[7] There are two axes in both family structures and narrative structures: in family structures, a vertical axis links parents to children and grandchildren through time, and a horizontal axis links siblings. Aunts and uncles, of course, move along both axes, first horizontally, to their siblings, then vertically, to their siblings' children. Similarly, each of these two narratives has two axes—one vertical, or moving through time, and one horizontal, existing within a single time frame. Let us look first at the relation between the familial axes and the narrative axes in the *Odyssey*.

The *Odyssey* is a story about inheritance, about the movement between the generations; it is a tale of transition between two periods, war and peace, and between two generations, those of Odysseus and Telemachos. If we accept this as a preliminary encapsulation of the subject of the *Odyssey*, then the work's final triumphant scene in Book 24 reunites the three generations represented by Odysseus's father Laertes, Odysseus himself, and Telemachos. This is a purely vertical transition, one between generations rather than between siblings: all the tension and anticipation and postponement of the *Odyssey* is released by this reunion between grandfather, father, and son.[8]

If we look more closely at family structures in the *Odyssey*, we find that one of its most remarkable features is that it is a work almost completely lacking in any lateral family relations—that is, brothers and sisters. Odysseus belongs to a line consisting of single sons,[9] and although he does have a sister, she is mentioned only once, very briefly, by the swineherd (15.361–65). Penelope sees a vision of her own sister once but it is only in a dream, and her sister's image disappears in a gust of wind (4.795–839). Bennett Simon points out that even the lies Odysseus makes up about himself once he has arrived in Ithaka have to do with the theme of brother-rivalry and thus reflect Odysseus's hostile attitude toward even invented siblings,[10] and I would argue that one of the reasons that Odysseus must lose all his shipmates and kill all his wife's suitors is that both of these two groups are potential brother figures (whether companions or rivals) in a narrative that abhors the fraternal.

If we return to Proust, we find that here, too, there is an astonishing lack of siblings. Marcel is an only child (whereas Proust had a brother), as are, apparently, his mother and father, Albertine, Gilberte, Swann, Odette, and Saint-Loup. Even the brothers and sisters that we do find are not always perceived as such: Legrandin goes to great lengths to conceal the fact that he has a sister near Balbec (1.129–33), while Marcel makes a tactless remark about the Duc de Guermantes, not realizing he is Charlus' brother (2.277–78).

In Proust's novel as well there is a close link between family axes and narrative axes, and the dearth of siblings in the novel might be partially explained by looking at the level of narrative structure. As in the *Odyssey*, we find in Proust a very strong vertical impulse, a desire to move between the generations rather than staying within a single generation. The narrator and the main character of the novel, even though they may in some respects be considered the same person, are not, after all, members of the same generation: there is a quantum leap to be made between the character Marcel, who spends his time dreaming about the day he will become a novelist, and the narrator writing his novel. We might consider this desire to become a novelist as the "goal" of the *Recherche*, a parallel to Odysseus's desire to arrive home and to connect the generations. Both works are centrally concerned with a transition between two eras, and it is within this impatience of the narrative to reach what it takes to be its goal that we may understand the paucity of the sibling relation, the horizontal relation that does not move one forward into the next generation.[11]

We might expect, then, that in the absence of the sibling relation, Proust's narrative would emphasize the parental axis, as the *Odyssey* does. But, in fact, not the least striking structural characteristic of the *Recherche* is that although it very rarely speaks of siblings, it is dominated not by the parental but by the avuncular. It would take a long time just to list all the aunts and uncles in the novel—those among minor as well as major characters—but here are just a few key ones: Marcel's Aunt Léonie,[12] who leaves him not only the heritage of the madeleine but also her money (1.454); Uncle Adolphe, who introduces Marcel to the *"dame en rose,"* or lady in pink (Odette); Charlus, who is both the nephew of Madame de Villeparisis and the uncle of Saint-Loup; and the Duchesse de Guermantes, who is Saint-Loup's aunt. Gilberte Swann becomes one of the richest heiresses in France by inheriting money from her father's uncle (2.747). The fact that Jupien's niece is sometimes referred to as his daughter, although certainly reflecting an incompletely corrected manuscript, also suggests that Proust had a fundamental hesitation about these two relations: aunts and uncles seem at some level to replace parents. Albertine Simonet lives not with her parents but with her aunt and uncle, the Bontemps. The first relative mentioned in the novel is neither Marcel's mother nor his father, nor even one of his grandparents, but rather his great-uncle, who tugs his childhood curls until the wonderful day when they are cut off (1.4), and even the crucial scene in which Marcel's mother reads to him all night in his bedroom (1.41–43) is preceded by the spiel ("boniment") that his great-aunt reads as an accompaniment to the images of the magic lantern (1.9). Moreover, a number of aunts and uncles in Proust's novel, such as Aunt Léonie, Swann's uncle, and Bloch's Uncle Nissim, leave money to their lucky nieces and nephews: they are "oncles à héritage" (1.773).

Indeed, when Marcel's mother goes to take care of her ailing aunt (2.1121–22), we see the avuncular relation continuing after the sororal one has ceased to function: this very aunt, Marcel's grandmother's sister, shirked her sisterly duty by refusing to visit the grandmother on her deathbed (2.325), and yet Marcel's mother, who "didn't like her aunt because she had not been the sort of sister for my grandmother—who was always so kind to her—that she should have been" (2.1121), nonetheless "wanted to bring her the consoling presence that my [great-]aunt had not come to offer my grandmother" (2.1122). The niece, by paying her respects to her aunt, seems to be making up for the latter's failures as a sister.

THE AVUNCULAR HERITAGE

Let us now turn back to Uncle Nissim and his Odyssean lie. One of the characteristics of the avuncular heritage in Proust is that it is thoroughly distinct from the paternal or maternal heritage—for the uncle or aunt, even though he or she may in fact leave money to surviving nieces and nephews, is not concerned about a successful transition between the generations, but rather lives only in the present. Thus Uncle Nissim is the quintessential uncle: when he lies, he does not worry about being found out one day. There are a number of variations on this single theme; that is, the novel's aunts and uncles escape the vertical generational movement in various ways, but escape it they do. Uncle Nissim, for example, resembles another prominent uncle in the novel, Charlus, through his sexual inclinations: both men are homosexuals, and since they have no direct descendants, they seem generally unconcerned about the future of the next generation. Aunt Léonie, although she is not presented as a homosexual, is nonetheless also childless, and so resistant to the idea of anyone's having children that she considers her peaceful routine to be fairly ruined by the kitchen maid's pregnancy (1.109).

The fact that the aunt's or uncle's perspective is lateral rather than direct is subtly demonstrated by Françoise's comment to Marcel after Aunt Léonie's death. Marcel points out that he feels no obligation to mourn his aunt, since "she could have been my aunt and seemed hateful to me" (1.154). Françoise's response to this is perhaps her single most meaningful mangling of French: "Just the same she was kin/parenthetical [de la parentèse], you still owe respect to kin/parentheses [la parentèse]" (1.154). Françoise confuses parenté, "kinship," with parenthèse, "parenthesis," and this confusion precisely describes the position of the aunt: a parenthetical parent, a parent figure pushed to the side, along the horizontal axis. The lateral displacement of the aunt or uncle is not simply indicative of a sibling relationship, but is also a displacement away from the center of interest and attention: the aunt is a marginal family member, one whose death need not be mourned since her story is only a parenthesis of family history.[13]

But although the uncle or aunt stands to the side of the parental axis—or, in Proust's terms, "de côté," one of the novel's key expressions—and thus exists outside of familial time, it is because of—and not in spite of—that lateral position that he or she can provide a narrative model. Uncle Nissim's lie has to do with the *conflict* between the familial axes and the narrative axes; the avuncular "lie"—existing outside of diachronic familial time—is a narrative truth,[14] and this is precisely what is demonstrated by the comparison of Uncle Nissim to Odysseus. Odysseus is called "the biggest liar in the world" just as he is returning to Ithaka in Book 13 of the *Odyssey*, and if he lies, *he lies as a father*—that is, in the interests of getting home in one piece and ensuring the continuity of his line into the next generation.[15] Uncle Nissim, by contrast, lies because he has no relationship to home—that is, no position along the diachronic familial axis; he lies for the pleasure of lying. Of course there is an element of pleasure in Odysseus's lying as well, as Roman Jakobson points out: Odysseus's lies may be seen as having an external goal (insofar as the goal of the epic is his safe arrival home) or as having no external goal (if we consider the *Odyssey* simply as an epic of story-telling).[16] But I would argue that Proust's comparison of the frivolous and fatuous Uncle Nissim to Odysseus is also an implicit contrast be-tween the latter's paternity and the former's avuncularity.

If Odysseus's "familial" lie has something lacking in Uncle Nissim's avuncular lie, then the question becomes this: what is the narrative truth that is involved in Uncle Nissim's lie and perhaps absent in Odys-seus's? The avuncular lie is in fact less a lie than the limiting case of one of the very principles of Proustian narrative: never to tell a story di-rectly. Seen in this perspective, the lie is merely an unusually indirect narration. Of Uncle Nissim's two reported "lies"—one stating that he is a senator and the other that he knows the Marquis de Marsantes—the latter turns out to be true some five hundred pages later (2.276–77), and although we are never led to believe that Uncle Nissim actually is a senator, Proust's narrative is so filled with shocking reversals of what we thought to be unshakable truths or bald-faced lies that such a reve-lation is certainly not beyond the novel's possibilities. The lie in Proust's novel—and, more specifically, the virtual impossibility of knowing with full certainty that it has no element of truth—teaches us that the question of truth in the narrative is intimately linked with that of postponement. Thus the avuncular lie is simultaneously an immedi-ate enjoyment of the present—made possible by the uncle's nonrelation to future generations and, by extension, to future time—and a post-ponement of judgment about the truth of things, a refusal to jump to hasty conclusions, whether logical or narrative. Familially, the avuncu-lar lie is out of time; narratively, it must be considered in time, indeed, as the very essence of Proustian temporality.

The avuncular heritage is thus much more than the fortune that rich aunts and uncles frequently leave to their nieces and nephews.[17] It is a moral model and a narrative model as well, or, more precisely, a con-flicting relation between a moral model and a narrative one. Perhaps the best example of this avuncular heritage is Uncle Adolphe, Marcel's grandfather's brother, the man who introduces Marcel to the beautiful and mysterious "lady in pink" who turns out to be Odette. Before mov-ing forward to the novel's second allusion to the *Odyssey*, let us look briefly at this famous scene between Marcel and Uncle Adolphe; in-deed, although there is no direct allusion to the *Odyssey* here, this scene is actually the first one in which Marcel receives hospitality outside his home.[18] To this extent the scene is a precursor of much of what follows, since a great proportion of the novel consists of Marcel's visits to various homes, and in this it is similar to the *Odyssey*. As a sort of miniature *Telemachiad*, the scene deals in a very subtle way with the question of the adolescent Marcel's identity, both moral and artistic, and more specifically with the relation between the moral or familial element of the avuncular heritage and its aesthetic or narrative component.

The entire scene is organized around the question of Marcel's avuncular heritage, since in the course of the scene we are told of three different family figures that Marcel might resemble: first his mother, then his father, and finally his uncle. When Marcel first arrives unannounced at his uncle's apartment, the lady in pink says that he looks like his mother ("Comme il ressemble à sa mère," 1.76); Uncle Adolphe counters by claiming that Marcel looks like his father ("Il ressemble surtout à son père," 76); and the scene ends when Marcel gallantly kisses the hand of the lady in pink and is rewarded by being told that he takes after his uncle ("il tient de son oncle," 78). But what is the exact value here for Marcel of "taking after his uncle"?

Uncle Adolphe is presented first of all as being morally "to the side," as taking his relations lightly and frivolously and not caring about the future, like Uncle Nissim:

> And if we went to see him only on certain specified days, that was because on other days he received women whom his family would not have been able to meet, or so at least they thought; for my uncle, on the contrary, the great ease with which he politely introduced pretty widows who had perhaps never been married or countesses whose thunderous names were undoubtedly made up to my grandmother, or even gave them family jewels, had already caused a number of family feuds between him and my grandfather. (1.75)

Uncle Adolphe makes a mockery of family relations and traditions: he frequents so-called widows who have never been married and gives away family jewelry on a whim; like Uncle Nissim, he does not give a thought to the future. Because he places himself outside of the temporal framework of the family, Uncle Adolphe embodies something of a "sideways" perspective on family relations, one that allows a certain amount of moral leeway.

One of the ways in which Marcel comes to resemble his uncle in this scene is that he allows himself to remove his moral blinders and take a good (sideways) look at the beautiful lady in pink. The metaphor of the blinders is given to us at the beginning of the scene, as Marcel sees Odette's carriage parked in front of Uncle Adolphe's building "hitched with two horses with a red carnation on their blinders ..." (75). On first seeing Odette inside Uncle Adolphe's apartment, Marcel does not dare "turn his eyes in her direction" ("tourner les yeux de son côté," 76); it is as if he himself were wearing the blinders. Thus, when he dares at last to kiss Odette's hand, the lateral movement away from the family—that is, away from its vertical impulse and from the axis that is concerned with the future—has been set into motion: Marcel resembles his uncle.

What is particularly interesting about this scene is that it presents Uncle Adolphe not only as a moral model of immediate satisfaction, but also as a narrative model of indirectness. Uncle Adolphe comes into his own in this scene, and he does so by discovering the power of oblique speech. Unlike his usual procedure of openly introducing his lady friends to the family without a second thought, Uncle Adolphe does not directly introduce Marcel and Odette: "My uncle said to her: 'My nephew,' without telling her my name, or telling me hers" (76). Although Uncle Adolphe's unwonted reticence here may appear to encompass an element of protectiveness—is he perhaps being avuncular in the usual sense by trying to protect Marcel from an open introduction to the scandalous Odette?—he undoubtedly fears the familial repercussions of such an introduction far more than any ill effects it might have on his nephew. And he once again proves himself worthy of being a Proustian uncle by telling Marcel to lie about the incident. Even this he does not say directly, but rather he hints to Marcel that it would be best not to tell his parents of his visit:

> While he [Uncle Adolphe] rather sheepishly implied [*me laissait entendre*], without daring to say it openly, that he'd just as soon I not speak to my parents of this visit, I told him with tears in my eyes that the memory of his kindness was so strong in me that one day I would find some way to show him my gratitude. It was indeed so strong that two hours later, after a few mysterious sentences that didn't seem to me to give my parents a clear enough idea of my newly acquired importance, I found it was more explicit to tell them in the most minute detail about the visit I had just paid. (79)

Marcel is not yet fully ready to receive Uncle Adolphe's avuncular heritage—or rather he is eager to receive its (im-)moral component but not its narrative component. His impatience to become an adult and thus to move into the next generation too quickly, reflected in his desire to display his "newly acquired importance" (that is, the fact that he has been introduced to an actress), is consistent with the moral element of the avuncular heritage, the need to satisfy one's whims immediately rather than following temporal norms; here Marcel is already worthy of his uncle. But he is not prepared to receive the avuncular heritage of narration, and this we see in his unwillingness to tell his story indirectly; the "few mysterious sentences" with which he first hints at his tale prove to be unsatisfying. The relation between the avuncular lie and indirect narration that we saw in the case of Uncle Nissim's tales is even clearer here: because Marcel, as soon as he is no longer in the avuncular presence, cannot for long resist telling his story *directly*, Uncle Adolphe is banished from the family forever (80).

The Avuncular Recognition Scene

What Marcel needs in order to become a narrator, then, is to recognize the complex nature of his avuncular heritage, both familial and narrative: to understand that he will always be out of order generationally and in order (although this order remains to be discovered) only narratively. Indeed, the next two allusions to the *Odyssey* in Proust's novel, both involving recognition scenes, culminate in the text's recognition of the avuncular and its lessons. In the first of the two, which occurs near the beginning of *Sodome et Gomorrhe*, Marcel watches the elaborate mating ritual of Charlus and Jupien:

> From the very start of this scene, a revolution had taken place in M. de Charlus that had opened my eyes, a revolution as complete, as immediate as if he had been touched by a magic wand. Until then, since I hadn't understood, I hadn't seen. Every person's vice (or so we call it for simplicity's sake) accompanies him like a genie invisible to humans so long as they are unaware of its presence. Kindness, deceitfulness, names, social contacts will not let themselves be discovered, and we carry them hidden. Odysseus himself did not at first recognize Athena. But gods are immediately perceptible to gods, as like is to like; so M. de Charlus had been to Jupien. Up until now, I had been watching M. de Charlus like a preoccupied man who, facing a pregnant woman whose heavy figure he has not noticed, listens to her cheerfully repeating "Yes, I am a little bit tired these days" and stubbornly, indiscreetly persists in asking her: "Well what's the matter?" But let someone say to him: "She's pregnant," suddenly he catches sight of her belly and will see nothing else from then on. (2.613)

Marcel's puzzlement is compared to that of Odysseus, who does not immediately recognize Athena, while Jupien and Charlus are compared to gods who recognize each other instantly. Once again, as in the scene with Uncle Nissim, we are dealing with uncles,[19] and, moreover, with uncles who are, like Uncle Nissim, homosexuals. The allusion is once more to Book 13 of the *Odyssey* and to Odysseus's first arrival on Ithaka. All these factors seem to suggest that in the nearly one thousand pages that separate the novel's first two allusions to the *Odyssey*, the relation of Proust's narrative to Homer's has gone nowhere.

There has in fact been a movement, but it is a backward movement, a movement away from home. Odysseus seems to have lost ground in his goal to arrive home; in the earlier allusion, Athena has already revealed herself to him, whereas this time he has not yet recognized her. Each of the subsequent allusions to the *Odyssey* will present increasingly serious challenges to homecoming, so that Proust's narrative will seem to read the epic in reverse, starting out with the promise of a homecoming and ending up dwelling on the obstacles to a completely satisfying return. The two homosexual uncles seem to be even more homeless than Uncle Nissim was: they are compared to gods recognizing each other instantly, while the slowness of Marcel's recognition of Charlus's true nature, which is compared to Odysseus's recognition of Athena, is consistent with familial temporality. The simile linking the two uncles' long-imperceptible homosexuality to the belly of a pregnant woman only emphasizes their childless (and homeless) state.

Thus uncles recognize uncles, or rather homosexuals recognize homosexuals,[20] but Marcel still has difficulty recognizing his own avuncular heritage, at least until the novel's next allusion to the *Odyssey*. In this passage, still in *Sodome et Gomorrhe*, we once again find two homosexuals who are "recognized" by an outsider: Charlus is dining with a footman dressed as an elegant aristocrat so that no one might suspect their liaison, and the first person to recognize the footman's true identity is Françoise:

> And even our old Françoise, whose sight was failing and who happened to be passing by the foot of the staircase just at that moment on her way to dine with the other servants, raised her head, recognized a servant where the guests of the hotel had no suspicion of one—just as the old nurse Eurykleia recognizes Odysseus well before the suitors seated at the banquet do. (2.988)

Françoise's instant recognition of the footman is compared to Odysseus's nurse Eurykleia who, in Book 19 of the *Odyssey*, recognizes Odysseus despite his rags because of a scar on his leg. Although this passage is further along in the *Odyssey* than the previous two—in fact, this is as close as Odysseus will come to his final family reconciliation in Proust's allusions to the work—the problems it raises for Odysseus's—or rather Marcel's—homecoming will provide the turning point for this intertextual reading.

For this allusion to the *Odyssey*, strategically as well as mathematically central (it is the third out of five), marks two key reversals: the novel's first two allusions speak of uncles either explicitly (Nissim) or implicitly (Charlus and Jupien), but its third allusion seems to leave the issue of avuncularity behind—for while Charlus is still involved, there is no hint that the footman might be an uncle (one suspects he is perhaps too young for this to be likely). But this apparent loss of avuncularity is the key to this passage, for we cannot simply consider the passage's relation to the forward movement of Proust's narrative, but rather must take a long sidestep into Homer's text. It is there that we will find the reappearance—and the true value—of avuncularity.

The scene alluded to in the *Odyssey* is without question the epic's single most important episode involving uncles. Let us first recall the context of the episode. Odysseus is back in Ithaka, but he remains in disguise and has revealed his identity only to Telemachos. He has just spoken at length to Penelope for the first time, and she orders the old nurse Eurykleia to wash him. The nurse recognizes a scar on Odysseus's thigh, and immediately knows him as her master. But this is the single longest recognition scene in the *Odyssey*, because of the long flashback narrative that describes several key events of Odysseus's early life—particularly how he got the scar that allows the nurse to recognize him. Thus, although this is the latest passage in the *Odyssey* to which Proust's novel alludes, it deals with the earliest events of Odysseus's life; one of the epic's few true flashbacks, it moves backward more than forward. Moreover, the recognition itself is immediate, but the scene that describes it is extremely protracted. The episode thus embodies both elements of the avuncular heritage—the immediacy of the present (the instant recognition, the most immediate in the whole *Odyssey*[21]) and the importance of postponement as a narrative technique.

In this, the longest of the *Odyssey*'s recognition scenes, we learn how Odysseus got his scar. When Odysseus was born, his maternal grandfather, Autolykos, promised that when he had come of age and was old enough to come visit his grandfather, he would receive many gifts. Odysseus does grow up, and in due time he comes to collect his gifts; but it is his maternal uncles rather than his grandfather who take Odysseus on a hunt. Odysseus's uncles are mentioned no fewer than seven times in the course of the narration of the hunt;[22] indeed, Odysseus gets his scar *because his uncles let him go ahead of them*, so that he is the first to come upon a wild boar. He aims his spear once, trying to hit the boar, but misses; the boar charges him and rips out enough flesh to leave a scar. Odysseus then lands a second spear shot, which kills the boar; his uncles catch up with him, dress his wound, take him back to their father's house, and send him on his way home with his gifts.

Thus, although Odysseus's gifts come from his grandfather, his scar comes from his uncles; it is *his* avuncular heritage. Odysseus gets the scar by going too fast: if his uncles had gone ahead of him to protect him as his father or grandfather might have done, he would never have received the injury, but because he is ahead of his uncles, he faces the boar alone. The hunt is Odysseus's rite of passage, his transition into the next generation, his coming into his inheritance—but nonetheless he is out of order. By passing ahead of his uncles, he not only (literally) puts himself in danger, but he also (figuratively) tries to move into the next generation too soon. Odysseus's speediness here is a metaphor for his impatience with time, his desire to grow up all at once—an impatience that is perfectly consistent with the moral element of the avuncular heritage that we have seen in Proust, the sidestepping of the normative forward generational movement. Odysseus's impatience is actually surprisingly similar to the impatience of the young Marcel who cannot wait to grow up and know actresses, like his uncle.

But if, as we have seen in Proust, the avuncular heritage has a narrative as well as a moral element, what does Odysseus's scar, his avuncular heritage, have to do with his gift for narration? Odysseus gets the scar between his first and second shots: had he killed the boar on the first shot, he would not have a scar, and he would not be recognizable as Odysseus. And the shot that is more interesting—that is, the one that gives rise to a narrative—is the shot that misses. When Odysseus returns home, the story he tells his parents is not about killing the boar, but rather about *not* killing it; he tells them not about the second, successful shot, but about the missed one: "Then his father and the lady, his mother, welcomed him back and asked him about everything, how he got the scar; and he told them thoroughly about how the boar with the white tusk caught him while he was hunting, when he'd gone to Parnassos with the sons of Autolykos" (19.462–66). Is this because, as Proust's novel tells us again and again, failures are infinitely more interesting (and make better stories) than successes? The archetypal boring narrative is that of a hunter describing a successful outing, and the model of an exciting one that of getting gored: as Odysseus's narrative proves, bagging a boar is a bore, while missing one makes for a riveting story (as well as a recognizable scar).

With this narrative lesson in mind let us return to Proust's text. The lesson of Odysseus's scar is that one's identity as a narrator is created as the result of an error, an initial failure to reach one's goal; that is, a postponement. If one did not make the mistake, one would never have the story. Proust's novel, like the *Odyssey*, reminds us repeatedly of the need to be sidetracked: if, as Erich Auerbach claims, Homeric digressions are not used to heighten tension and suspense but rather are meant to be enjoyed in the same degree as the parts of the story that seem to move the narrative forward,[23] then Proustian "error"—missing the mark, not reaching the goal, or even being disappointed if ever one does arrive at it—is the very essence of narrative avuncularity. Being outside of the parental order is what allows one access to the avuncular order of narration.

In fact, this lesson drawn from the *Odyssey* is *more applicable to Proust's work than to Homer's,* and this crossing over between the two texts essentially defines their intertextuality; it is the (perhaps subconscious) need for this avuncular lesson that pushes Proust's text toward Homer's and motivates the series of allusions we are examining. The allusion to Odysseus's scar is the watershed of our intertextual reading, the point that sends the two texts off on their respective courses, Odysseus toward home and Marcel toward an ultimate recognition of homelessness. For although Odysseus's avuncular heritage allows him to return home (albeit ten years late), he must shed that heritage before he can complete his homecoming, as we shall see. But for the protagonist of Proust's novel, the avuncular heritage comes to replace home; the homelessness that it implies is an inescapable element of Proust's narrative.[24]

The Nonparental Narrative and the Parental Nonnarrative

Thus Proust's final two allusions to the *Odyssey* deal with the failure of direct, vertical links between the generations. Both these allusions are to the *nekuia*, the scene of the conjuring of the dead in Book 11 of the *Odyssey*; we thus leave Odysseus not only farther from home than when we found him, but also in the part of his journey that most emphasizes loss, the irretrievability of past generations through anything other than narrative.

Both of these final two allusions to the *Odyssey* take place near the end of *Le Temps retrouvé*, at the famous scene of the matinée Guermantes, when Marcel is just about to sit down (or so he claims) to start his novel. In the first allusion the narrator describes seeing an old friend:

> I found there one of my old chums, someone I used to see almost every day for ten years. Someone offered to reintroduce us [*à nous représenter*]. So I approached him and he said to me in a voice that I recognized perfectly well: "What a pleasure to see you after so many years!" But what a surprise for me! His voice seemed to come from an extremely accurate phonograph, for if it was my friend's voice, it came from a fat, graying chap that I didn't know. . . . Still I knew it was he: the person who had introduced us after so much time hadn't been the slightest bit mysterious. . . . I tried to remember. In his youth he had blue, perpetually laughing eyes, always mobile, obviously in search of something. . . . But now, since he had become an influential politician, capable and despotic, his blue eyes, which by the way hadn't found what they were looking for, had become immobilized. It certainly seemed to me that he was someone else, when suddenly . . . I heard him laugh, and it was his silly laugh from the old days, the one that went with the perpetually merry mobility of his look. . . . Then the laugh stopped; I would

have liked to recognize my friend, but, like Odysseus in the *Odyssey* rushing up to his dead mother, . . . I stopped recognizing my friend. (3.941–42)

What identifies Marcel's friend for him is the searching look he always had in his eyes as a young man; without this look, which he has by now lost, he is virtually unrecognizable. Marcel has a moment of recognition when his friend laughs, since Marcel associates his laugh with the searching look ("his silly laugh . . . that went with the perpetually merry mobility of his look"), but when the laugh stops, the recognition stops as well. This searching look is thus doubly a link between the generations: first, because it allows Marcel to recognize his friend across the years, to connect the old man to the young man he once was; and second, because what the young man was looking for, the object of his own "recherche," is, we presume, what propelled him into the future. It is in this light that we may interpret the man's having lost his searching look, since by reaching the next generation (that is, by growing old), he has achieved (or perhaps forgotten) the goals of his youth; he has nothing left to search for.

Thus when the friend's laugh stops and Marcel stops recognizing him, this does not mean that Marcel no longer knows the man's identity; indeed, his singularly unavuncular introduction ("the person who had introduced us after so much time hadn't been the slightest bit mysterious") leaves no room for doubt on that score. Rather, it means that when the friend stops laughing and thus loses the final vestige of his old searching look, Marcel can no longer really believe this is the same man he knew. What we are being told is that there is no stable, recognizable link between the generations, between Marcel's friend as a young man and as an old man. The searching look allows Marcel to move through time, to recapture the past momentarily—but only momentarily. The poignancy of Proust's scene results from the difference between the two meanings of "représenter": to represent is not simply equal to "re-presenting," or presenting again, as when Marcel and his old friend are reintroduced to each other; rather, representation as a part of narration cannot continue to provide a successful link between two time periods.

If Marcel is to connect the generations by becoming a narrator, then this narrative link must be an *alternative* to the parental link, and it is at this point that we must examine Proust's comparison of Marcel to Odysseus and his mother. Odysseus, in the underworld sequence in Book 11 of the *Odyssey*, sees his mother and discovers that she died from missing him. The two exchange stories but they cannot embrace, for she is only a shade, and when he wants to hug her she tells him that it is impossible, and that he should instead observe the ghastly scene of the dead so that he can tell stories about it to Penelope later on (11.223–24). Storytelling is presented here as a kind of supplement to mortality; by telling the story of his dead mother to Penelope, Odysseus supposedly makes up for not being able to hug her and thus bring her back from the dead. Regulated generational passage is of course also a strategy against mortality, an attempt to compensate for individual mortality through the link of familial continuity; as a different sort of supplement to mortality, storytelling provides an alternative to this link. For Odysseus, to tell the story of the underworld is to narrate his desire to be reunited with his mother in the domain of the living, his desire to make her present to him once again; but also the impossibility of satisfying that desire.

The limitations of the parental axis are clarified in the novel's final allusion to the *Odyssey*, which appears a little later in the same scene of *Le Temps retrouvé*, when Marcel sees Odette again. His reunion with the "lady in pink," without his Uncle Adolphe, nonetheless teaches him an eminently avuncular lesson:

> Because she hadn't changed, she hardly seemed alive. She looked like a sterilized rose. I said hello to her, she looked for my name on my face for a few moments. . . . I said my name and immediately . . . she recognized me and began to speak to me with that voice. . . . But still, just as her eyes seemed as if they were looking at me from a distant shore, her voice was sad, almost begging, like the voice of the dead in the *Odyssey*. . . . I was the one who had in earlier days gone such a long way to catch a glimpse of her in the park, the one who had listened to the sound of her voice fall from her lips, the first time I had been at her house, like a treasure; but the minutes I now spent with her seemed interminable to me because I couldn't figure out what to say to her, and I went away telling myself that Gilberte's words when she said "You've confused me with my mother" were not only true, but that it was quite generous of the daughter to say them. (3.950–51)

Odette is no longer the "dame en rose," the rose lady who prefigures the "jeunes filles en fleurs" or flower girls of the narrative, and speaking to her now is a sterile experience. It is sterile, paradoxically, because she herself represents the possibility of making a smooth, trouble-free transition between the generations, and this transition is exactly what the narrative cannot—or will not—provide.

There are a number of reasons why Odette is boring here: she has not suffered or struggled over the relation between the generations (this is undoubtedly why she appears unchanged); she has given birth to a daughter who now takes her place; she can even be confused with that daughter. How Odette ultimately lassoes Swann into marriage and family might, in very broad terms, be one way to summarize "Un

Amour de Swann"—and that story is fascinating from Swann's side (precisely because it is, from his point of view, the story of a failure) and quite boring from Odette's (because it is, for her, a success). If we think back to our familial axes, it is the story of how Odette, Uncle Adolphe's lady in pink, went "straight"; as she is no longer a *cocotte*, there is no need to take one's blinders off to look at her now. Odette looks like "a sterilized rose," which might sound puzzling, since she has in fact given birth to a daughter. But this metaphor reflects Marcel's perspective here. Even though the narrator never completely loses his desire to connect the generations, that desire is constantly displaced by the impossibility (or perhaps the refusal), narratively speaking, of making that connection directly.

It is in this light that we can explain the allusion to the *Odyssey* in this scene. There is something very puzzling here: Odette is compared to the dead who vainly implore Odysseus to allow them to speak; Marcel should then be Odysseus, the master of the word. But in Proust's scene it is Odette who speaks (at great length, moreover) and Marcel who says nothing. Is this not a way of implying that Odette's speech is not real speech, or rather that it is not narration? If Odette's speech leaves Marcel at a loss—"I couldn't figure out what to say to her"—does his silence not mark the final evolution of the avuncular lie that began our intertextual reading? The avuncular lie, as we have seen, is an indirect narrative, and Marcel's silence here can be considered both a rejection of Odette's purely "parental" speech and a signal of his own (avuncular) narrative-to-come.

END OF AN ODYSSEY, BEGINNING OF A *RECHERCHE*

How, then, does Marcel become a narrator? This is the Proustian equivalent of the question of how Odysseus arrives home and stops being a narrator, for Marcel arrives home only insofar as he becomes a narrator, and what he will be narrating will be a "nonhome," whereas Odysseus must put an end to his tales in order to complete his homecoming. This double question of the ending of the *Odyssey* and the beginning of the *Recherche* seems to be a reassertion of the parental axis in this relation of intertextuality, for it is the question of how to close the narration of the "parent" text and begin the narration of its "offspring." But the avuncularity of our intertextual reading teaches us quite a different lesson, and in order to demonstrate this I would like to conclude with one final parallel, which is based on the entire narrative situation of the *Odyssey* and of Proust's novel; in both cases, this narrative situation will take us back to the questions of the avuncular heritage and avuncular intertextuality.

The place where Odysseus tells his story at greatest length is in Phaiakia, to King Alkinoos and Queen Arete, and I think it is not a gratuitous detail that King Alkinoos is *his wife's uncle* (7.63–68), for the entire sequence in Phaiakia takes place under the sign of the avuncular. King Alkinoos actually *acts like a Proustian uncle*: he offers his daughter in marriage to Odysseus embarrassingly too soon (7.311–15; it is only the fourth speech he makes to Odysseus, who is, after all, a perfect stranger). Odysseus, by the same token, answers him in a manner worthy of Uncle Adolphe: he never actually responds to the offer, but by not answering he merely hints (just as Uncle Adolphe insinuates [*laisse entendre*]) that he would rather go home to Ithaka. Even Alkinoos's marriage offer has an avuncular element. The temptation of Uncle Alkinoos is that of denying the forward passage of time by marrying a woman who is a generation younger than her husband. This Alkinoos has done by marrying his niece, and he offers a similar prerogative to Odysseus: to marry Nausikaa, Alkinoos's daughter, a young girl. This would of course mean never returning to Ithaka, the story's destination, so that the uncle's offer attempts to disrupt the narrative's momentum.

But even more striking than this avuncular disruption in the realm of what the Russian formalists would call *fabula* (the order of events referred to by the narrative) is the avuncular disruption in the domain of *sjužet* (the order of events as they are presented by the narrative discourse). Odysseus, as he tells his story to an uncle and a niece, interrupts the momentum of the narrative: he refuses to tell the events of his story in correct chronological order. He starts out with the most recent past (his years with Kalypso), and then goes back to the fall of Troy and narrates his adventures chronologically until he returns to Kalypso. At this point he refuses to repeat the story of Kalypso: "I hate repeating a story when it has already been well told" (12.452–53); these are the famous lines that end the first half of the *Odyssey*. One of the reasons Odysseus does not repeat the end of his story is that if he did so, the events of the entire story would be in the right order, and his story would be over. The narrative strongly suggests that Odysseus cannot tell the story straight until he gets home.

In fact, among the different occasions on which Odysseus tells his tale in the work, the only time he does so completely chronologically is once he is home with Penelope (23.310–43), when the forward impulse of the narrative has been satisfied; moreover, this final narration marks the end of the act of narration in two ways. First, Odysseus ends his story with the journey from the Phaiakians' island to Ithaka, a trip during which he is asleep, and as he is narrating this, he falls asleep himself: in the act of narrating, he is doing the same thing that is going on within the story itself. It is actually impossible to tell if Odysseus's slumber is within the tale or within the act of narrating it: "Then he said the last word, when sweet relaxing sleep came upon him, loosening his care-bound spirit" (23.342–43). Is the "sweet relaxing sleep" the last word of the story itself—Odysseus's journey home, asleep, with the Phaiakians (13.79–80)—or does it come once he has actually finished telling the story? Since he falls asleep telling a story about falling asleep, we cannot say: the very act of narration seems to disappear, to be absorbed by the events described in the narration. The second way that the act of narration is shackled here is that Odysseus's final tale to Penelope takes the form of the narration of a narration: we get not Odysseus's words, but rather the narrator's words telling of Odysseus's narration ("then godlike Odysseus told everything, how . . ."), and this is undoubtedly because if Odysseus himself were given the floor, the storytelling impulse would win out over the homecoming impulse. This narration at a double remove encloses Odysseus's narration within another, controlling narrative; once again, the narrative impulse is subordinated to the demands of homecoming.[25]

As we turn back to the *Recherche* one last time, the question then becomes this: given the collapse of the parental axis of narration that we saw in the novel's final two allusions to the *Odyssey*, how can Marcel initiate his narrative? If the parental impulse, the movement toward the next generation, demands that Marcel reach the goal of starting the novel, he still has not done so at the end of the novel. How, then, do we move from the realization of the limitations of the parental to the beginning of the narrative?

If the end of the novel marks the failure of the parental axis, we must go beyond the end and back to the beginning in order to witness the final reception of the avuncular heritage. I would like to suggest that when one reads this novel a second time—which its cyclical nature requires—the novel does not "start" until the beginning of the narration of the madeleine episode, since the passage leading up to the madeleine scene is essentially a continuation of the problem, left over from the end of *Le Temps retrouvé*, of how to begin the novel. As in the *Odyssey*, the frame story involves sleeping, since the narrator seems to start out trying to write his novel by going to sleep and dreaming about his life. But even at the beginning of the novel, which chronologically follows the end, he is in fact still not writing the novel, as the continuous narration does not begin until after the madeleine episode. Perhaps he first tries to write it during the day, and tries so hard that he falls asleep early ("Longtemps, je me suis couché de bonne heure"). If he falls asleep trying to tell the story in this way, it is that he is still trying to be Odysseus, who does after all fall asleep after he tells his story straight: he is attempting to start his narrative purely along the parental axis, trying both to reach his own past in a direct way and to follow the narrative model of the *Odyssey* as a parental text.

He corrects this false start by doing two things: first, he narrates how he lost forward time to begin with—that is, the story of the night his mother spent in his room, the roots of his moral avuncular heritage. The lesson of that night is, as Marcel realizes too late, that he gets what he wants *too soon*: spending the night with his mother is representative of moving into the next generation before the time is right. Marcel, like Odysseus in the hunting scene, *wants his grandparent's gifts ahead of time*, as his mother points out: "Will you have less pleasure if I already took out the books your grandmother is going to give you for your feast-day? Think hard: are you sure you won't be disappointed when you get nothing the day after tomorrow" (1.39)? This is a metaphor for Marcel's entire misadventure with time: he will always be either too soon or too late, and he will never have anything the day after tomorrow; the future will bring no gifts. Marcel in his impatience has no uncles by his side as Odysseus did (although let us recall that he has already been read to by his aunt), but he is henceforth in the avuncular position, the position of existing outside of "family" time.

The second thing Marcel does to "correct" the forward impulse of the parental axis is to narrate the source of the narrative avuncular heritage, the madeleine episode: for it is in this episode that *Aunt Léonie comes to be substituted for Marcel's mother*. Marcel starts the episode suffering from his moral avuncular heritage, "weighed down by the mournful day and the perspective of a sad tomorrow" (1.45), at odds with time. But out of this experience of lost time is born the avuncular heritage of narration. As soon as Marcel recognizes what the memory of the madeleine is, the memory of his Aunt Léonie's section of the house comes to replace that of his parents' wing at Combray. The subsequent description of Combray takes place mainly in Aunt Léonie's wing, and is the story of her *traintrain*, or little routine, her own refusal and rejection of forward time. Odysseus cannot tell his story "straight" so long as he is in the house of an uncle, but Marcel cannot begin to tell his story crookedly (that is, at all) until he is in (and under) the wing of his Aunt Léonie.

Moreover, if Odysseus's homecoming is punctuated by the narration of a narration that marks a kind of bracketing of the act of narration, Proust's narration begins with the memory of a memory, the experience of the madeleine epiphany that is, more precisely, a voluntary memory of an involuntary memory. When Marcel tries to start writing the novel by remembering all the different rooms in which he has ever slept, he is using memory as a way of trying to gain direct access to his past, to reconstitute a real home; here he is moving along the parental axis. He realizes that none of these rooms is "home" in the sense that Odysseus has a home, when he remembers how he lost home, by losing a normative relationship to the passage of time (the good-night kiss). And finally he *remembers* the madeleine epiphany—which is not, as some critics have claimed, either out of chronological order or completely undefined chronologically, but rather simply *in the order of Marcel's memories*, the next memory he has in his attempt to begin the novel. And this is the memory that works where the others failed, precisely because it pushes him simultaneously off the parental axis and away from voluntary memory—and in so doing signals their inability to initiate the narrative.

Thus, in spite of all the emphasis that has (rightly) been placed on the role of memory in Proust's novel, I would like to suggest that the initiating moment of the narrative requires going against memory as a simple mechanism of homecoming, a direct link between past and present, and asserting the lateral power of the avuncular narrative. When Marcel remembers the experience of eating the madeleine with his mother and being reminded of Aunt Léonie, he is pushed off the parental axis (his mother, remembered voluntarily) and to the side (his Aunt Léonie, remembered involuntarily); indeed, the reappearance of Aunt Léonie, although it may seem to provide a pure link with the past, immediately recreates a world "beside" Aunt Léonie, the world of Combray to which she is contiguous (or, rather, which is contiguous to her) (1.47–48). What Gérard Genette might call the metonymization of the metaphorical experience of the madeleine[26] shows that its value depends not on an isolated backward movement, but rather on a simultaneous backward and sideward motion. The parental impulse of reaching the goal of starting the novel is thus neither simply reached nor simply lost; rather, it is vectorized, pulled to the side: the parental impulse—that is, the moment of beginning the narration—is paradoxically concomitant with an avuncular recognition. In the very act of beginning to narrate his novel, Marcel simultaneously links the generations (the relation between character and narrator) and is made to realize that the narration itself will be one of a nondirect link between the generations, a story worthy of (and under the auspices of) Aunt Léonie.

This is the moment that marks the final "avuncularization" of the intertextual relation, the moment at which Homer's text loses its temporal priority and its parental status. At the center of our intertextual reading we found a crossing-over, an exchange between two texts, Proust's text drawing from Homer's an avuncular lesson that in some respects it needs more than Homer's does. After this avuncular recognition, the Odyssean intertext in Proust dwells on the failure of the parental axis, as we have seen. Indeed, once the exchange between the two texts has set the intertextual reading into motion, the texts begin *to read each other*; the ultimate collapse of the parental axis takes place not only within Proust's text itself, but also in the relation between the two texts. What started out in the form of a parental relation—a series of allusions establishing a link to a text seen as prior—becomes a consanguine relation of adjacency and substitutability.

This final infraction of normative intergenerational temporality by which the *Odyssey* seems to engage in an *exchange* with a text three thousand years its junior is yet another lesson of avuncularity (as well as of intertextuality): the impossibility of completely separating the closure of one generation and the initiation of another, the *overlapping* of the generations that at times allows nieces and nephews to be older than their aunts and uncles. The *Odyssey* joins its inner story and its frame story by ridding itself of the avuncular narrative heritage: Odysseus's final story to Penelope is not only told in the right order, but it is also the story of a successful journey: not the story of the scar, but the story of killing the boar. Maybe that is why it makes him fall asleep—it is, told in this way, actually rather a boring tale. But if the *Odyssey* seems, in discarding its avuncular heritage, to pass it on to the *Recherche*, this does not make of it a parental heritage, for Proust's text itself defines that heritage by reading Homer's: the avuncular heritage of intertextuality is never passed on simply between the generations, since it is as much a heritage from an "heir" to its ancestors as one that moves in the usual forward direction. It is a heritage that never ceases to try to equalize the texts between which it moves, to set them side by side. So that when Marcel begins to tell his story, he is able to do so because he has at last come into his avuncular heritage—but the reception of this heritage does not mean, as most heritages would, that a stable relation between the generations has been established. A haunter of houses rather than an inhabitant of one, the narrator will never simply move between past and present. And this is why he starts his narration by telling us not about the house he is in, and not about a house he might be moving toward, nor even about the houses he has been to, but rather about a house he has been *beside*: *Du côté de chez Swann*.

Chapter 2

T(R)YPTEXT:

PROUST, MALLARMÉ, RACINE

NOVEL, LYRIC, TRAGEDY

THE STARTING POINT of this chapter is a literary triple-cross-roads that Proust sets up at a key moment of his novel. Marcel writes a letter of adieu to the recently departed Albertine, telling her that had she not left him, he would have asked for her hand in marriage and given her a yacht and a Rolls-Royce, but also making it clear that he will not ask her to come back.[1] In the text of this letter Marcel quotes fragments of two sonnets by Mallarmé: he tells Albertine that her yacht would have been called "Le Cygne," or "The Swan," in honor of one of Mallarmé's poems, "Le vierge, le vivace et le bel aujourd'hui," the hero of which is a swan, and that on the Rolls-Royce he would have had engraved the final two tercets of another Mallarmé sonnet, "M'introduire dans ton histoire." The intertext immediately established by the letter is one between Proust's monumental novel and two short Mallarmé sonnets, made even shorter by their quotation in abbreviated form. But this first intertext is placed within a larger context that establishes an equally important intertext between Marcel's letter and a famous passage in Racine, the scene of Phèdre's confession of love to Hippolyte (*Phèdre*, 2.5). Marcel gives his letter to Françoise to mail, but he neglects to tell her how many stamps to put on it. When she brings it back to him, he launches into a detailed analysis of Phèdre's confession scene before he finally makes a firm decision to send the letter, drawing a lengthy analogy between his own uncertainty about whether he actually wants his message to be delivered and Phèdre's mixture of terror and desire at the thought of revealing her love to her stepson (3.458–60). Thus the Mallarmé intertext, which has to do with the body of the letter, is inextricably linked to the Racine intertext, which establishes the conditions of delivery of the letter, the question of whether it will ever be sent.

It is my premise that this crucial moment in Proust's novel constitutes not two separate intertexts, but rather a single conjunction of three texts. Proust's novel brings together Mallarmé and Racine, thus establishing a triple relation: that of Proust's text with Mallarmé's, that of Mallarmé's with Racine's, and that of Proust's text with Racine's. It is far from coincidental that the three texts in question represent radically different genres: novelistic prose, lyric poetry, and tragic theater. If, as Bakhtin puts it, "the novel gets on poorly with other genres,"[2] we may wonder why Marcel needs not only two other texts to write (and to decide whether to send) his letter, but also two other "types" of texts.

The notion of "t(r)yptext" is thus based not only on a *triple* conjunction of texts, but also on a triple meeting of *types* of texts. This concept of literary types is partly drawn from Christian typology, which, by attempting to establish a relation between Old Testament and New Testament texts (that is, "types" and "antitypes"), is an early and particularly powerful example of an intertextual system. Indeed, as we shall see, some of the main tensions in the works of all three of the authors in question can be understood in terms of the relations between the Old and the New Testaments. And although intertextuality, unlike Christian typology, is not explicitly a moralized system, intertextual readings often implicitly follow the model of typology by creating the impression that the intertext provides a previously hidden solution to problems posed by the text. The underlying assumption of this kind of intertextual criticism is that it is linear and progressive: as the Old Testament type is related to the New Testament antitype, as the partial is related to the complete, or the prefigurative to the fulfilled, the text is related to the intertext.[3]

But my main goal in using the model of typology is in fact to *distinguish* literary typology from theological typology. I would like to demonstrate that the intertextual relation between the three literary "types" that I will examine does not provide articulations between them in a movement of progression. Rather, literary typology makes us aware of the characteristics, distinctions, and limitations of each of the types involved without deciding between them. Just as it is absolutely essential that Swann falls in love with someone who is not his type (1.382), texts of different types need something from one another: in this particular instance, Proust's novel cannot reach the climax of its failed love story without a sort of interrogation of the strategies that might be brought to the conflicts at hand by lyric poetry and tragic theater. That interrogation does not establish the superiority of Proust's own type, but simply explores the nature of all three of the types involved without any notion of hierarchy or relative moral value. The "avuncular" intertextuality we explored in Chapter 1 had to do with the difficulty of linear progression between Homer's text and Proust's (as well as the impossibility of linear progression within Proust's text itself). Similarly, the intertextual relation we will examine in this triple (rather than the more usual double) juxtaposition of texts is not linear—composed of a clear unidirectional or even bidirectional movement from one text to another—but rather nodal—composed of a multiple crossing of the ways.

PROUSTIAN TYPOLOGY

Before considering the intertext linking Marcel's letter to both Mallarmé and Racine, let us define the importance of Christian typology for Proust's own text. Several critics, led by Proust himself, have recognized that Marcel's and Albertine's relationship provides so many clear parallels with that of Swann and Odette that the novel's two love stories appear to be based on a sort of typology: Swann and Odette are but a type to which Marcel and Albertine will provide an antitype. As Georges Cattaui puts it: "*Du côté de chez Swann* . . . is a kind of prefiguration, or Old Testament, since Marcel's and Albertine's relations will be the repetition and resumption of the love and jealousy shared by Charles Swann and Odette de Crécy."[4] Similarly, Marcel Muller speaks of the "typological opposition between the Jew [Swann] and the Gentile [the narrator]" in which Swann "functions as a representative of a 'Judaic' reading of reality" and he and the narrator are linked by a movement of progression that "leads from the imperfect to the perfect . . . as in any truly typological relation."[5] As the Old Testament is related to the New Testament, "Swann in Love," the story of Swann's and Odette's slowly evolving relationship, culminating in a marriage—under mysterious circumstances—that does not come until some time after the end of that section of the narrative, is related to Marcel's and Albertine's liaison, resulting in nonmarriage. Let us look more closely at some of the issues involved in this Proustian typology.

Why does Swann fall in love with Odette? And why does he finally marry her? The answer to both of these questions is the same: because of his relation to time, one of the keys of Old Testament narration. Before meeting Odette, Swann's "loves" are mere infatuations limited to an endless present tense devoid of memory. Swann is like a pre-Abrahamic nomad: "He did not close himself into the edifice of his relations, but had made of that edifice—in order to reconstruct it all over again from scratch anywhere where a woman pleased him—one of those collapsible tents that explorers carry along with them" (1, 192). Not only explorers, but also nomadic tribes travel from place to place carrying tents, and in fact the wanderings of the Hebrews provide one of the central motifs of the Pentateuch. Starting off from a position in which wandering is synonymous with nonmemory and nonhistory, the people who will ultimately become the Hebrews—although to some extent they never stop wandering—become wanderers with a memory, their history one of wanderings, their minds and spirits ever turned not only toward God's promise of entry (or return) to the land in the future, but also toward the past history of that endlessly postponed promise. When Swann falls in love with Odette, he does so through the acquisition of memory: he slowly begins to anticipate their rendezvous and finds that he so enjoys anticipating them that he postpones them more and more until the day he misses Odette entirely and finds her absence intolerable (1.226); this is the night their relationship is consummated. Swann thus desires Odette either in the future tense or in the past tense—he postpones their visits but is anguished at having missed her—but not in the present tense. He values her insofar as he cannot truly possess her in the present, the act of love being an act by which "one possesses nothing" (1.234).

Odette becomes a kind of promised land, not a true homeland to which one finally comes, but rather the anticipation (and memory) of a home of which one will never be sure, a sort of lesson in the formation of a temporal and historical perspective. David J. A. Clines's description of the central topic of the five books of Moses thus equally applies to Swann's feelings for Odette: "The theme of the Pentateuch is the partial fulfillment—which implies also the partial non-fulfillment—of the promise to or blessing of the patriarchs."[6] The Hebrews come to value the Promised Land precisely because of the difficulty of possessing it in the present tense; one of the reasons they cannot enter the land for many generations after it has been promised is that their relation to it must be historicized. Thus when God promises Abraham that he will give the land of Israel to Abraham's descendents, his promise is first stated in the future tense ("eten et haaretz," "I shall give the land," Genesis 12.7; "etnena," "I shall give it," 13.15), and then in the past tense ("natati et haaretz," "I have given the land," 15.18); not only is the promise not stated in the present tense,[7] but it is stated in the past tense long before it has come to pass. The promise (to be fulfilled in the future) itself becomes historicized—it becomes a history of promises— many hundreds of years before it is fulfilled. Analogously Swann's love does not reach its apogee of development until he has lost Odette, that is, until she no longer loves him; it is a function of his historicization of their relationship—and more specifically of the time during which he actually did *not* love her, but the memory of which is one of the major constituting elements of his love for her once he feels he has lost her—and of his desire to secure her promise of fidelity in the future. Swann is obsessed by Odette only insofar as she is not in his presence, or at the very least makes him feel at every moment that she could be, will be, and has been with others: his liaison with her becomes the pure potential for faithfulness or infidelity. Like the Hebrews' relation to the Promised Land, it is a kind of locus of testing.

It is no surprise, then, that Odette becomes associated in Swann's mind with Zephora, Moses' wife (1.222), for Swann becomes Moses, the leader of the Israelites who himself is not allowed to enter the Promised Land. As Clines says: "We are left at the end of the Pentateuch, at a point of tension or expectation: the goal of the journey has not been reached, and Israel's leader [Moses], the dominant human figure since the beginning of Exodus, is dead. Israel's future is open-ended, even perhaps in jeopardy."[8] Moses is emblematic of the Hebrews' relation to the Promised Land: he can lead them to it, he can keep their desire for it and their memory of its promise alive, but he can no more enter the land himself than he can guarantee that his people will ever possess it in an unconditional present tense, without remembering the tenuousness of their possession. "Swann in Love" is the story of Swann's being tamed, not by Odette, but by a recognition of the nature of human mortal time: the severe limitations of the present and the consequent need for a relation to time and history.

Thus the essential opposition of "Swann's way" and the "Guermantes way," the two symbolic walks that the young Marcel takes at Combray and that come to represent "deep mines of my mental soil" (1.184), has to do with two distinct relationships to time and history. Swann's way is about the uncertainty of time, the dangers of change and fluctuation and cycles. The walk along it is taken on days when the weather is threatening, when the sky could change at any moment— just as the young Swann changes women constantly, and his father, an "agent de change" (1.16), has a peculiarly intermittent memory.[9] The landscape is that of a plain, the site of agricultural and animal cycles, the site of desire, whence comes its relation to Sodom and Gomorrah, the cities of the plain, later in the novel. When Marcel first sees Gilberte on a walk along Swann's way, she is carrying a hoe, the agricultural tool that penetrates the soil and prepares it for the planting of the seed (1.140). Just as the weather is constantly changing along Swann's way, the cycles of nature bespeak the acute problems of time and variability raised by the Pentateuch from the moment of the fall from Paradise.[10] In both the five books of Moses and "Swann in Love," the "solution" to the problem of time is not geographical, but temporal: not the Promised Land as such, but rather an awareness of the promise and its tenuousness, an awareness of the need for memory—a relation to time— over and above any conceivable certainty about possessing it. Swann's way is the way of the Pentateuch.

Along the Guermantes way, by contrast, time is not a problem. This walk is taken only on days of stable, fine weather. The landscape is bordered by a transparent river, the Vivonne, which represents an unencumbered, flowing relationship to time. The fish that are repeatedly mentioned as inhabiting the river are symbols of Christ and Christianity, and the fisherman whom Marcel meets is the only figure in the region of Combray whose name he never learns (1.167); he is devoid of a secular identity. Similarly, we are told of anonymous ladies who come to the countryside to forget their unhappy loves (1.170–71). The Guermantes way is the way of forgetfulness (or nonmemory), time along it sempiternal and unchanging.

When, in the final scene of *Le Côté de Guermantes*, the dying Swann brings the Guermantes an enormous photograph of a medallion of the order of Saint John of Jerusalem (2.574, 585–93), this reminiscence of the Crusades and of the Christians' attempt to take possession of the Holy Land is not a sign of Christianization but rather a final, implicit expression of Swann's Judaism—"coming to the premature end of his life, . . . [Swann] was returning to the fold of his fathers" (2.581)—in the face of the Guermantes's Christianity: the Crusaders' seizure of Jerusalem, that is, their need for land, is, in the context of Swann's way and the Guermantes way, a sort of taunt, Swann's implicit "I-told-you-so" to the Guermantes. Swann seems to be saying that in a certain era even Christians felt the need to possess the Promised Land. It is no coincidence that Swann's enormous photograph cannot fit through the Guermantes' door (2.593), for what it represents—the enormity of history, the need for posterity precisely because of the impossibility of possession in the present tense—cannot be assimilated into the Guermantes' "way" (of life). The photograph corresponds to the irremediability of death: both the Duke and the Duchess refuse to confront Swann's imminent death, announced in this scene. What is important here is that there is a close relation between the recognition of death and loss on the one hand and the need for posterity on the other: the Guermantes, of course, have no children.

Swann finally marries Odette because of his desire for posterity: because of their daughter, Gilberte, who is born well before the marriage and is generally recognized as the reason for it (1.23, 466–67). The relation between Swann's need for posterity and his status as an Old Testament figure is borne out by the possibility that Gilberte is born during a "croisière" or cruise to the Middle East, a sort of modern-day *croisade* during which Odette symbolically takes possession of Swann by bearing his child in his absence. Gilberte's conception is part of Odette's plan to snare Swann. Long after they have ceased relations, she comes to him, frenetically, and asks him to make love to her:

On certain evenings she suddenly showed her old kindness toward him, but harshly warned him that if he did not take advantage of it immediately, he might not see it come back again for years; he had to accompany her home immediately and "make *catleya*," and this desire for him that she claimed to have was so sudden, so inexplicable, so imperious, . . . that her brutal and unlikely tenderness saddened Swann as much as a lie or an unkind act. (1.372)

Odette's "inexplicable" desire for Swann, as well as its uncompromising and crucial timing, become easily comprehensible if we realize that she is simply trying to get pregnant. Odette soon leaves on her cruise, which is supposed to last for only a month but goes on for a year, finally reaching Constantinople (1.374). I would argue that it is during this cruise that Gilberte is born; this would explain why Madame Cottard, upon meeting Swann after her return to Paris from the cruise, mysteriously hints at a reconciliation between Swann and Odette (1.376). How else can we explain that reconciliation, which must take place some time between the end of "Swann in Love"—at which point Swann is fully out of love with Odette and seems to have no plans of seeing her again (1.382)—and the time of their marriage some years later?

Now to return (at last) to Marcel's letter to Albertine, it is because that letter expresses Marcel's doubts about marrying his lover that it is at the crux of the relationship between the Old and the New Testaments. Insofar as the text makes it plausible—although never verifiable—that Albertine's entire relationship with Marcel (like Odette's with Swann) may be reducible to her willingness to sell her love (a spiritual thing) for marriage to a socially prominent man, Albertine is a potential perpetrator of "simony" (her surname is "Simonet"). Although Albertine is not Jewish, Jeanne Bem argues convincingly that she is in a position of "Judaity" ("judéité");[11] a certain number of signs make her identity assimilable to that of a Jewess, a potential confusion that is linked to her family's insistence on the distinctness of the "Simonets" and the "Simonnets," some of whom, one surmises, might be Jews.[12] If, as Muller claims, Proust's narrator is really a New Testament figure, Marcel's letter to Albertine thus precludes the potential repetition of the essentially Old Testament outcome of Swann's relationship with Odette; his rejection is necessary if Marcel's and Albertine's love story is to be distinguishable as the antitype of Swann's and Odette's. By not marrying Albertine, Marcel is refusing to found a lineage, to establish a posterity.

PROUST/MALLARMÉ: *HISTOIRE DU SWAN(N)*

Given its status as an antitype, it is inaccurate even to call Marcel's and Albertine's relationship a love "story," because this is the point at which Proust's text refuses to consecrate itself as the story of "Un

Amour de Marcel." It is with this in mind that we may once again approach the question of why Proust has recourse in the text of Marcel's letter to two texts of Mallarmé's. What exactly are the messages conveyed by these two poems? What does it mean for Proust to turn to Mallarmé at this crucial juncture of his novel? And what is the message of lyric poetry that Proust's novel is trying to appropriate?

"Le vierge, le vivace et le bel aujourd'hui" is a poem about the necessity of migration, about the need to establish "une région où vivre," or "a region in which to live." The unspoken biological premise of the sonnet, which describes the death throes of a swan frozen into the ice of a lake in winter, is that the swan is a migratory bird. This is a poem about a swan who for some reason did not migrate with the others in his flock.

Thus the "cygne," the hero of the poem and also the name of the yacht imagined by Marcel, is more than eponymously related to the "Swan(n)"—with two *n*s rather than one, like the Simonnet family, and thus himself under the sign of "Judaity"—of Proust's novel. The "swan," like Swann, is defined by a problematical relation to time, for the swan, too, realizes that time has a dangerous capacity for obscuring one's potential: "Un cygne d'autrefois se souvient que c'est lui / Magnifique mais qui sans espoir se délivre . . ." [A swan of former times remembers that he is the one / Who is magnificent but gives himself up without hope . . .][13] The despair of the swan, the beginning of his death scene, is set off by an act of memory, and memory for the swan, as for Swann, comes from a realization of time's potential for loss.

But the swan's death is the moment that sets him apart from Swann, for ultimately Marcel's friend, by marrying Odette in the name of his posterity, accepts the establishment of a household as the human equivalent of the swan's need for migration. For the swan, migration would not be a sign of aimless wandering, but rather a giving in to the needs of mortality, the acceptance of spatiotemporal regulation for a creature who, without time and history, cannot have access to any form of permanence.

To this extent what is remarkable about Mallarmé's sonnet is that it, too, might be considered to stand at the juncture of the Old Testament and the New Testament, for the death of the swan is followed by what appears to be a kind of resurrection, the appearance of the Swan who ends the poem and might be thought to be an idealized, nonincarnated, and nonmortal version of the swan, perhaps even the swan's soul. The "exil inutile" or useless exile that is the condition of this Swan contrasts with the swan's lack of a "région où vivre," for the exile is useless precisely because the idealized Swan has no need of home: as a kind of

New Testament antitype to the earlier swan's type, he is "home" nowhere and everywhere; his very nature is defined by a relation to eternity rather than to secular time.

Thus the lesson of the first poem that Marcel quotes here is a lesson of nonposterity; it seems to offer Albertine—or rather Marcel—a vehicle for escape (like the imaginary yacht named after it), a nonmarriage, a New Testament response to Swann's Old Testament solution to the problem of time. But the second Mallarmé poem quoted here complicates this intertext considerably. Let us begin our discussion of this second, less well known sonnet by quoting it in its entirety:

> M'introduire dans ton histoire
> C'est en héros effarouché
> S'il a du talon nu touché
> Quelque gazon de territoire
>
> A des glaciers attentatoire
> Je ne sais le naïf péché
> Que tu n'auras pas empêché
> De rire très haut sa victoire
>
> Dis si je ne suis pas joyeux
> Tonnerre et rubis aux moyeux
> De voir en l'air que ce feu troue
>
> Avec des royaumes épars
> Comme mourir pourpre la roue
> Du seul vespéral de mes chars.

[To get myself into your story / It is as a hero scared off / If with his naked heel he touched / Some territorial grass / I don't know of any innocent sin / Attempting to assault glaciers / That you will not have prevented / From laughing its victory out loud / Say if I am not joyful / Thunder and rubies at the hubs / To see in the air that this fire bores through / With scattered kingdoms / The wheel, purple, as if dying, / Of my only chariot of evening.]

The poem is about a man's thwarted desires at the moment of sunset: his wish to enter into his lover's "histoire" (that is, to have a "love story" with her, "histoire" also being a sexual metaphor), his being rebuffed, his fear of having trespassed on her "territory" by his desires, and finally his wistful observance of the sunset (the descent of the "chariot of evening" with its ruby-red glow). The sunset is itself a complex metaphor of, simultaneously, mortality as the precondition of desire ("Comme mourir pourpre la roue"), the sexual act itself ("l'air que ce feu troue"), and the failure (or rejection) of desire in this abortive "love story"; that failure leads to a nonterritoriality ("des royaumes épars," the scattered reddish purple clouds of sunset suggesting a dispersion of royal wealth).

The problems raised by the sonnet are similar to the issues of Proustian typology: posterity (the mortal cycle of desire, procreation, and death) as a strategy against temporality (Old Testament) versus a rejection of the love story and of history ("histoire" in both cases), that is, of procreation and posterity, with a consequent lack of territoriality (New Testament). To this extent "M'introduire" seems to give Marcel the same message as the Swan sonnet: the swan's refusal to migrate—leading to his death and resurrection in an idealized form, outside of secular time—is parallel to the "hero" kept out of his lover's "histoire." Moreover, the absence of the masculine rhyme of the two quatrains, "-ché," caused by Proust's truncated quotation of the sonnet suggests the very absence of posterity and homing—"*chez*," as in *Du côté de chez Swann*—embodied by Marcel's rejection of Swann's "solution" to temporality. Thus far the two sonnets are in agreement in rejecting the "Swann" principle.

But there is an important difference here, one accentuated by the misquotation of the sonnet within the text of Marcel's letter. The first two lines quoted are reversed: "Tonnerre et rubis aux moyeux / Dis si je ne suis pas joyeux," rather than "Dis si . . . / Tonnerre . . ."[14] This inversion draws attention to the single line that, from the perspective of our reading, most differentiates this sonnet from the Swan sonnet: "Dis si je ne suis pas joyeux . . . ," the imperative, presumably addressed to the lover, upon which the entire second half of the poem depends.

The importance of this line is that it demands a response from the person to whom the poem is addressed. This is a gesture extremely untypical of Mallarmé: while many of his poems are addressed to a female "tu," that "tu" generally remains "tu," or silenced (Mallarmé himself uses this pun more than once). What the poet is asking his resistant lady is nothing less than to establish the value of the whole scene that occupies the second half of the poem: because she rejects his advances, he watches the sunset that itself seems to him to reenact the human drama of mortality and desire, and when he asks her to tell him if observing this drama makes him joyful (or, by implication, sad), he is asking her to tell him the value of the human drama of the need for posterity. Whereas the Swan sonnet rejects temporality, "M'introduire" poses the question of temporality, and leaves that question unanswered.

This appeal to a "tu" gives the poem itself a temporal element that is usually lacking in lyric poetry. Lyric generally creates a fleeting mood or expresses the feelings of a moment; it has no extent in time. As Barbara Hardy puts it in contrasting Shakespeare's Sonnet 104 ("To me, fair friend, you never can be old") with Proust's novel: "The poem . . . does not express duration or ageing as Proust takes time to do; [in the sonnet] these are instruments by which the central feeling can be registered."[15] Mallarmé's sonnet, by asking for a response, takes on an incipient theatrical element: it is as if the poem were attempting to go beyond its form—lyric poetry supposing the expression of a moment rather than a dialogue developed across time—by ending with a question without whose answer we are scarcely able to establish the mood of the sonnet ("Tell me if I'm not happy").

Thus in "M'introduire," Proust finds a literary type that itself is at the juncture of the three types in question in this chapter: lyric poetry, prose, and theater. As we have seen, the poem is a rejection of "histoire" as both love story and sexual act—a rejection that seems to tell Marcel to end his own potential love story with Albertine—but the sonnet also reaches toward theater, since the failure of the "histoire" leads to the poet's demand of a response from the woman to whom his message is addressed. Perhaps it is this demand of a response, as much as the sonnet's notorious obscurity, that makes Albertine claim not to understand this poem (3.456). And it is this very hinge position between lyric and dramatic poetry that will lead us to the next phase of our reading.

MALLARMÉ/RACINE: *CANTIQUE DE (SAINT) JEAN (RACINE)*, OR, TRAGEDY AND LYRIC

As we have seen, Proust embeds his quotation of Mallarmé's poems within a letter whose delivery he makes dependent upon a text of Racine's, the confession scene in *Phèdre*. In so doing, he establishes a relation not only between his own text and those alluded to, but also between Mallarmé's poetry and Racine's theater. In fact the two writers Proust brings together in a single intertextual node are not utterly foreign to each other; rather, this conjunction is in itself extremely fruitful. In examining this relation between Mallarmé and Racine in the light of the issues raised by Proustian typology, we are not leaving Proust's text behind but rather following its lead; as we shall see, this relation will provide a necessary link that will ultimately lead us back to Proust's novel.

Although Mallarmé is one of the central figures in the nineteenth-century renaissance of lyric poetry, his interest in theater is well known, and the Tournon crisis, the crucial early period that was influential in forming him into a mature poet, coincides with his rejection of theater as an impossible expressive outlet for him: the early projects of

"L'Après-midi d'un faune" and "Hérodiade," both conceived for the theater, evolved into long poems. Mallarmé's poetry has a remarkable affinity with tragic theater, and more specifically with the dramatic poetry of Jean Racine. Not only did Mallarmé continue to be interested in theater during much of his life, but he predominantly wrote in the alexandrine, and, as different as his use of the form is from Racine's, he too brings it to a kind of pinnacle of development within a verse that creates an impression of purity, restraint, and perfection. As A. R. Chisholm puts it, "Mallarmé's form is almost wholly classical. . . . [He] applies to the romantic data of his century a method that is really classical."[16]

The single poem that brings Mallarmé closest simultaneously to Racine, Proustian typology, and the question of the intersection of tragedy and lyric poetry is "Hérodiade." Conceived as a tragedy, for the theater, the poem evolved during the Tournon crisis, between March and November of 1865, from "my tragedy of *Hérodiade*" (*Oeuvres complètes*, 1440) to "*Hérodiade*, no longer a tragedy, but a poem" (1442). Moreover, it retains certain traces of its heteroclitic development, since the poem as it appears in the Pléiade edition of Mallarmé's complete works[17] is made up of three distinct parts: an opening monologue ("Ouverture") in which the Nurse sets the scene by describing Hérodiade's flight from her bed and early-morning wanderings; a scene between Hérodiade and the Nurse, the central action of which is the Nurse's questioning of her charge about the possibility of her marriage; and the short poem "Cantique de Saint Jean," spoken by John the Baptist at the moment of his decapitation, presumably after Salomé (or perhaps Hérodiade) has requested his head from Herod. The poem itself is thus a triptych, and as such it will help us to explore further the concept of a "tryptext," a text based on a triple conjunction of texts of different types.[18]

The "Hérodiade" triptych is, like "M'introduire dans ton histoire," a failed story. As Wallace Fowlie points out:

> The central question asked by the nurse: "for whom are you keeping yourself?" is not answered, or answered enigmatically, when Hérodiade says, "for myself." What might have become a story, reminiscent of a famous myth, is interrupted, and we are plunged into a shadowy world of a mirror, the dominant symbol of the poem.
>
> But by the very title of his work, the strong resonant name Hérodiade, Mallarmé forces his reader to think of a biblical story, alluded to by Saint Mark and Saint Matthew. . . . Or, more simply, more mysteriously, does he want us to think of his princess as a "heroine" because the name begins in its first two syllables with "hero"? Might Hérodiade be Salomé, who is unnamed in the two accounts of *Mark 6* and *Matthew 14*?[19]

The failure of "Hérodiade" to be an *histoire* is based on a double rejection of normative temporality; its heroine's refusal to instigate a love story by accepting a lover or husband, and Mallarmé's refusal to make his tragic poem into a "story." If Hérodiade's status as heroine depends on her clinging to her unchanging, virginal state, this suggests that the "héros effarouché" of "M'introduire" is a hero only *insofar as* he does not have a successful "histoire."

Both Hérodiade and the "héros effarouché" of "M'introduire" have strong Racinian resonances. Fowlie compares Hérodiade's refusal of sexuality to the forbidding chastity of the Greek Hippolytus (as well as to the swan of "Le vierge, le vivace"),[20] and although Racine portrays Hippolyte at the moment of his sexual awakening, the single most famous description of him in *Phèdre*, one that comes in the very scene analyzed by Proust, preserves his innocence and identifies him, too, as "farouche":

> Oui, Prince, je languis, je brûle pour Thésée.
> Je l'aime, non point tel que l'ont vu les enfers,
> Volage adorateur de mille objets divers,
> Qui va du dieu des morts déshonorer la couche,
> Mais fidèle, mais fier, et même un peu farouche,
> Charmant, jeune, traînant tous les coeurs après soi,
> Tel qu'on dépeint nos dieux, ou tel que je vous voi.

> [Yes, Prince, I am languishing, I am burning for Thésée. / I love him, not as the underworld saw him, / The fickle worshipper of a thousand different love-objects / Who intends to dishonor the bed of a god, / But faithful, and proud, and even a little wild, / Enchanting, young, carrying off everyone's heart, / Just as our gods are portrayed, or just as I see you.][21]

The "farouche" Hippolyte is the "héros effarouché" of Racine's play, and in the light of "Hérodiade" it is particularly interesting that Phèdre's description of him as "farouche" comes in a speech that confuses his identity with his father's in such a way as to undermine the concept of posterity. For Phèdre is not describing her stepson simply as his father's heir in the realm of love; rather, she moves backward in time by making the aging, corrupted father resemble the son ("Il avait votre port, vos yeux, votre langage"; "He had your bearing, your eyes, your language," 641). Like Hérodiade, she refuses the cycles of life initiated by a sexual rite of passage.

Perhaps the most interesting point of contact between "Hérodiade" and *Phèdre* is that both works are based on a series of temporal conflations that resist the passage between the generations and thus demonstrate the difficulty of constituting a posterity, a difficulty that is a key feature of tragedy as a literary type. The scene between Hérodiade and her nurse finds its closest parallel in Phèdre's confrontations with her own nurse, Oenone,[22] but Hérodiade herself is, as we have seen, at least as much an Hippolyte figure as a latter-day Phèdre, the intergenerational collapse between stepmother and stepson being in this case doubled by a collapse of sexual difference particularly appropriate in a figure who refuses all sexuality. Moreover, the vagueness of the identity of Mallarmé's heroine—is she actually Salomé, the young daughter of Herodias, or Herodias herself?—also conflates two generations. And, as we have seen, this double conflation in Mallarmé's poem finds its analogue in Phèdre's own assimilation of Thésée to the youthful Hippolyte. In all three cases, the instability of the generational difference expresses a heroic refusal of the passage of time, a wish to bring time to a halt.

The relation of this tragic rejection of posterity in Mallarmé's poem and in Racine's play to our triple conjunction of literary "types" becomes clear in the short poem that forms the third part of Mallarmé's triptych. The speaker in the poem is John the Baptist at the moment of his decapitation, which Mallarmé places at the summer solstice—very near the Feast of Saint John (June 24)—the high point of the summer sun. This setting appears at first to make the poem conform to a familiar Mallarmé model: a "solar" poem, in which the permanence and autonomy of the sun contrast with the mortality and contingency of a mortal observer.[23] The saint's death at first seems nothing more than yet another escape from the need for posterity. If this is so, the "goal" of the decapitation is simply to stop the sun:

Le soleil que sa halte
Surnaturelle exalte
Aussitôt redescend
    Incandescent

[The sun which its supernatural / Halt exalts / Immediately comes back down / Glowing]

The sun stops momentarily to mark the horror of the Baptist's execution as it does at certain portentous moments of biblical narration (and also as it appears to do at the solstice, which means "sun stoppage"), then continues its inevitable descent beyond its apogee; but the Baptist, because of his decapitation, does not see this falling-off. When his head is separated from his body at the instant of the solstice, his death may be seen as a result of the tragic conflict between the heroic attempt to stop time and the cycles of mortality.

But this tragic, heroic reading of the poem, prepared and suggested in a sense by the first two parts of the triptych, is ultimately misleading. I would like to suggest that the Baptist's death, or, more specifically, the poem as his ultimate utterance in death, participates in a different type: that it is not a tragic, heroic death but rather a lyrical one.

Indeed the three parts of the poem, although they are all in verse and the first two both use alexandrines, are of three different types: the "Ouverture," which sets the scene and prepares us to expect the story of Hérodiade to be told or acted out, is essentially a third-person narration of events; although the Nurse does use the first-person singular once, it is precisely in order to call her own voice into question: "Une voix, du passé longue évocation, / Est-ce la mienne prête à l'incantation?" [A voice, long evocation of the past, / Is it mine ready for incantation?] The second part is the scene itself, a theatrical exchange between two characters that climaxes in Hérodiade's rejection of posterity. The final section brings yet another type into the poem, for John the Baptist, the "I" of the poem, addresses a "you"—the "glaciers," which are a figure for the coldness and the purity of the heavenly absolute[24]—not theatrically but rather lyrically, at a distance, without expectation of a response:

> Qu'elle [la tête] de jeûnes ivre
> S'opiniâtre à suivre
> En quelque bond hagard
>   Son pur regard
>
> Là-haut où la froidure
> Eternelle n'endure
> Que vous le surpassiez
>   Tous ô glaciers

[May it (the head) drunk with fasting / Persist in following / In a kind of haggard bounce / Its pure look / Up there where the eternal / Coldness does not endure / Your surpassing it / All of you glaciers]

Saint John's utterance implies a heavenly audience, but one that will not answer back, the "vous tous ô glaciers" that are extremely important as a link between all of the Mallarmé poems we have examined. In the "Ouverture," the Nurse speculates that the "glacier farouche" that reflects the arms of Hérodiade's absent warrior-hero father in battle is ignorant of Hérodiade's melancholy: "Son père ne sait pas cela, ni le glacier / Farouche reflétant de ses armes l'acier ..." [Her father does not know this (Hérodiade's solitary sunset walks), nor does the wild /Glacier reflecting the steel of his weapons ...] The "glacier farouche" is the witness of the father's heroism as a victory over death, and the father is utterly cut off from his daughter's drama: here again, heroism is an alternative to posterity. Similarly, the "transparent glacier" underneath the virginal surface of the frozen lake in the Swan sonnet is the potential for procreation and generation that the nonmigratory swan will never realize—what more poignant image of nonbirth can one imagine than these "vols qui n'ont pas fui," or flights that haven't taken flight?—while the "glaciers" that the "héros effarouché" assaults in "M'introduire dans ton histoire," a metaphor for the woman's resistance and remoteness, once again result in nonprocreation and thus an absence of posterity.

However, in "Cantique de Saint Jean," these "glaciers" are the "vous" of the poem, and here they are not described as "farouche" (like Hippolyte); they are not figures of heroic ambition, or of refusing the passage of time and the falling-off it implies. Rather, the poem takes us to the interstices between lyric poetry and theater, for it brings us back from the essentially heroic conclusion of the "Scène" to a lyric expression of a single moment; it is because the Baptist's words are addressed to an unhearing, unresponsive audience of "glaciers" that his utterance takes on a lyrical value.

It is tempting to consider this as the moment of Mallarmé's own arrival at a sort of antitype. Undoubtedly countless readers have been struck by a certain element of disembodiment in Mallarmé's poetry, a deemphasis on the physical presence of anything or anyone,[25] and this disembodiment is in fact in strong contrast to his earlier poems, a number of which—"Une Négresse" and "Tristesse d'été" are two striking examples—have a very marked, disturbing corporality that gives one the impression that, to quote one of Mallarmé's most famous lines, "La chair est triste, hélas!" This uneasy physicality is particularly apparent in "Don du poëme," which is based on a metaphor linking the writing of a poem with childbirth: "Je t'apporte l'enfant d'une nuit d'Idumée! / Noire, à l'aile saignante et pâle, déplumée..." [I bring you the child of an Idumaean night! / Black, with a bleeding, pale wing, plucked...] According to Charles Mauron, the poem being born in "Don du poëme" is "Hérodiade";[26] Mallarmé was working on "Hérodiade" at the time "Don du poëme" was written, and Hérodiade is an Edomite or Idumaean princess (the child of an "Idumaean night"), a descendant of the ruddy ("edom," red) hunter Esau, an Old Testament figure. The birth described in "Don du poëme" is a very physical, bloody birth, and if we accept Mauron's interpretation, "Cantique de Saint Jean" could be read as a sort of Christian antitype (redemption through decapitation, the relegation of the body in favor of the soul) to the type of "Don du poëme" (the pain and difficulty of birth into mortal existence); Saint John's death, a joyful relegation of the life of the body in favor of that of the soul, puts an end to "Les anciens désaccords / Avec le corps" [The age-old discords / With the body].

Thus the poem ends with John's "baptism" in his own blood:

Mais selon un baptême
[La tête] Illuminée au même
Principe qui m'élut
    Penche un salut.

[But according to a baptism / (The head) Illuminated by the same / Principle
which elected me / Bows a salvation (or greeting).]

Baptism is itself an antitype, a rebathing in the waters of the flood of
Genesis that marked the first of many attempts to purify the human
soul. Rather than a return to the land (the founding myth of Judaism),
it is a return to the primordial waters that figure timelessness; it is not
an acceptance of the powers of death but a denial of those powers, a
redemption or salvation ("salut") in death: the Baptist quite literally
baptizes himself in death.

Nevertheless, as tempting as this sort of typological reading might
be, I have indulged in it largely in order to suggest its limitations.
"Cantique de Saint Jean" will provide us with an important bridge
between Christian typology (the movement between type and antitype) and literary typology (an interaction of literary types). As Paul de
Man points out, "a theme that recurs constantly in all the *Tombeaux*
poems" is Mallarmé's "opposition against a conventional Christian notion of death as redemption."[27] If this is so, Mallarmé would appear to
reject one of the very premises, the concept of salvation—French
salut—upon which Christian typology is built. But it is this very word,
salut, a word that both ends the "Cantique" and opens Mallarmé's col-
lected poems ("Salut" is the title of the first sonnet in the collection),
that will provide the articulation between Christian and literary typology, for the word has two separate meanings: it can be either a pon-
derous theological term (salvation) or an informal greeting (hello or
goodbye). I would like to suggest that at the end of "Cantique de Saint
Jean," the Baptist is saved less in a Christian sense than in an aesthetic
sense: he is "saved" by the movement into lyric, the literary type that
Mallarmé is here recognizing as his own by relegating—perhaps re-
gretfully—the more temporally based dramatic poetry of tragedy. This
literary typology requires Saint John to make a quick bow and take
his leave lest his lyric poem become too long and enter into the domain of temporality (and thus tragedy): at the end of the poem Saint-
John's "salvation" ("salut") comes from simply nodding goodbye
("salut").[28]

It is through the very issue of salvation that this third part of "Hérodiade" bears as important a relation to Racine as do the first parts of
"Hérodiade" through their parallels to *Phèdre*. I would like to suggest
that the "Cantique de Saint Jean" also has a Racinian intertext, and a
lyrical one at that. We must not forget that just as Mallarmé was a failed

tragedian who wrote lyric poetry, Racine was a lyricist as well as a tragedian: he wrote a number of odes, "cantiques spirituels" based on various biblical texts, and verse translations of hymns from the Latin breviary. The verse form of the "Cantique de Saint Jean," with its rhythmic pattern—unique in all of Mallarmé's poetry—of 6–6–6–4 in each stanza, could be scanned as a variant of the 12–10 pattern favored by Racine in some of his own "cantiques." More specifically, perhaps the most famous of Racine's lyric poems, his translation of a hymn for Tuesday matins, "Verbe égal au Très-Haut,"[29] realized its full lyrical potential in the very year that saw Mallarmé set to work on "Hérodiade" and give up his ambition to make it into a tragedy: in 1865 "Verbe égal" was set to music by the young Gabriel Fauré—one of the main models for Proust's Vinteuil!—under the title "Cantique de Jean Racine" (Opus 11). Even if we overlook the remarkable coincidence by which Racine carried the name of John the Baptist (his full name was, of course, Jean-Baptiste Racine), the timelessness at the center of Mallarmé's "Cantique de Saint Jean," as well as the poem's peculiarly Racinian verse form, fittingly echoes the lyrical Racine, just as the "Ouverture" and the "Scène" echoed the tragic one. For the lyrical Racine, too, tries to escape the cycles of temporality in his own lyric addressed to a Christian time-out-of-time:

> Verbe égal au Très-Haut, notre unique espérance,
>> Jour éternel de la terre et des cieux,
> De la paisible nuit nous rompons le silence:
>> Divin Sauveur, jette sur nous les yeux.

[Word equal to the highest, our only hope, / Eternal day of the earth and the heavens, / Of the peaceful night we break the silence: / Divine Savior, cast your eyes upon us.]

But just as Mallarmé's turning toward tragedy leads to a reaffirmation of lyric as his own literary type, Racine's lyric poem—even though it is simply a translation—cannot sever its author's ties to tragic issues. Although the form of Racine's poem is lyrical, as a liturgical text it is preoccupied by its reception, and this challenges its status as lyric:

> Répands sur nous le feu de ta grâce invincible (puissante);
>> Que tout l'enfer fuie au son de ta voix;
> . . . .
> O Christ sois favorable à ce peuple fidèle
>> Pour te bénir maintenant assemblé;
> Reçois les chants qu'il offre à ta gloire immortelle;
>> Et de tes dons qu'il retourne comblé.

[Spread over us the fire of your invincible (powerful) grace; / May all of hell flee at the sound of your voice; / ... / O Christ show favor to this faithful people, / Gathered now to bless you; / Receive the songs it offers to your immortal glory; / And may it come back showered with your gifts.]

The speakers in the "cantique" participate in a (potential) exchange, for if God receives it, they seem to expect a favor—no less than salvation— to mark its reception; the savior's voice is written into the poem ("au son de ta voix"). In fact this "cantique" drew criticism for Racine's phrase "grâce invincible," which was considered to reflect a Jansenist overemphasis on the role of divine grace in the salvation of the soul; Racine's son and biographer, Louis, substituted the phrase "grâce puissante" precisely in order to sidestep critics. This modified text, which Fauré adopted in his musical setting, is more idiomatic to lyric: it praises the power of God's grace ("grâce puissante"), while Racine's "grâce invincible" places grace in a context that underlines its ultimate effect upon humanity, what the Jansenists would call its *efficacité*. And as we know at least since Lucien Goldmann's work on the absent (and present) God in Racine,[30] as soon as we are dealing with the relation of God (or gods) to humans in Racine, there is no question of simply praising God: we have entered into the realm of tragedy. The "cantique" brings us back to the intersection between lyric and tragedy, for it is around the very issue of the gods' reception or nonreception of a message that we will find the articulation between lyric and tragedy in Racine's most famous play, and it is by way of that articulation that we will return to Proust's text.

RACINE/PROUST: LYRIC, TRAGEDY, NOVEL

Since we began by allowing Proust to bring Mallarmé and Racine together, let us now use Mallarmé to bring together Proust and Racine. For just as the intersection between Mallarmé and Racine is to be found along the line separating—and connecting—tragedy and lyric, the passage in *Phèdre* that Marcel analyzes in *La Fugitive* will allow us to examine the articulation between lyric and tragedy within Racine's most famous play, the very play to which, moreover, both "M'introduire dans ton histoire" (with its "héros effarouché") and "Hérodiade" send us.

Phèdre's problem is that she inhabits a tragic rather than a lyrical universe. Her message—the irresistibility of her illicit love for Hippolyte, which Oenone rightly points out is a sign of her mortality ("Mortelle, subissez le sort d'une mortelle" [As a mortal, accept the fate of a mortal], 1302)—is ultimately made to arrive rather than being expressed from afar. Hippolyte, like the *glaciers* to which Saint John addresses his lyrical swan song, is certainly "glacial": the effect that uttering his name has on Oenone is one of icy horror ("tout mon sang dans mes veines se glace!" [all of my blood is frozen in my veins!], 265), and Aricie speaks of his almost legendary coldness ("Je sais de ses froideurs tout ce que l'on récite" [I know all that is said about his coldness], 405). But unlike the remote and unhearing *glaciers*, Hippolyte is finally made to hear Phèdre's lament, and this is what compromises her own heroic stance, her decision to commit suicide rather than give in to Venus's challenge.

Phèdre thus brings us to the intersection of tragic theater and lyric poetry from the opposite direction to "Hérodiade," as a tragedy that implicitly looks toward, but ultimately cannot appropriate, the model of lyric. The play's central problem is not how to make oneself understood, but rather how to speak without being heard; how to relieve oneself of the burden of one's emotions without having that unburdening become a part of the drama's complex of events—that is, without having it enter into a temporal network. Phèdre has no regrets about telling Oenone of her love for Hippolyte ("Je t'ai tout avoué, je ne m'en repens pas" [I've admitted everything to you, I'm not sorry I did], 312), but she is ultimately made to rue the arrival of her message at its destination, Hippolyte. Phèdre recognizes the vital distinction between speaking and being heard, the sending and the delivery of one's message. She never seems to regret that she has revealed what she has revealed, but only that her revelation was heard: "J'ai dit ce que jamais on ne devait entendre" [I've said what should never have been heard] (742).

If Phèdre could address the expression of her sorrowful love to a remote, unresponsive listener, this would make her plight not more cruel but rather more bearable. But this is not a lyrical, atemporal universe, and her message reaches not only Hippolyte's ears but also those of her controlling goddess, Venus. Hippolyte himself, the immediate receiver of Phèdre's message, is repeatedly compared to the gods: Phèdre calls him "ce dieu que je n'osais nommer" [this god that I dared not name] (288), so that naming him becomes akin to apostrophizing the gods: "Hippolyte? Grands dieux!" (264). Even in speaking to Hippolyte Phèdre compares him to the gods: "Tel qu'on dépeint nos dieux, ou tel que je vous voi" [Just as our gods are portrayed, or just as I see you] (640). Hippolyte's reception of Phèdre's message leads to the sending (and the disastrous receiving) of her message to an actual god. Phèdre prays to Venus that Hippolyte might fall in love ("Qu'il aime" [Let him love], 823), an utterance that itself loses its lyric potential when it is answered, that is, sent back to Phèdre, in a slightly (but crucially) altered form: "Qu'il l'aime" [That he loves her (Aricie)] (1188), the phrase by which Phèdre learns the news that Hippolyte is in love, but not with her. The added direct object, a single letter ("l'"), is perhaps the most economical example of an ironic tragic response in the history of theater. Phèdre's "héros effarouché," when he hears her message, does "introduce himself into her story," or rather she catastrophically introduces herself into his; what might have been a moving adieu in a lyric poem becomes the dangerous moving force for the rest of the drama.

In his analysis of *Phèdre* Proust's narrator focuses on this key transition in the play, the moment when Phèdre, by making Hippolyte receive her message, loses the possibility of keeping her expression of love a pure lament. Proust seizes *Phèdre* at the moment it loses its lyric potential and transforms itself into a tragedy. Whereas the problem of the transmission of Marcel's "Mallarméan" letter, a problem centered around the Mallarmé/Racine intertext, is about the relations between tragedy and lyric, Proust's analysis of *Phèdre* will provide an articulation between tragedy and Proust's own aesthetic type, the novel. Let us look at the terms of this transition from Racine's tragedy back to Proust's novel.

The immediate cause for Proust's analysis of Phèdre's confession is the announcement of the death of La Berma, the tragic actress whom Marcel has seen play Phèdre several times and whose manner of playing the role he has understood in various ways. Now I would like to suggest that the death of La Berma coincides with the moment at which, through the analysis of Phèdre's scene, Proust's novel essentially rejects its tragic potential, and more specifically its tragic relation to time.[31] If the strategy of tragic heroism in the face of temporality is, as we have seen in both "Hérodiade" and *Phèdre*, the attempt to stop the passage of time, then the reason Marcel has been disappointed throughout his life is that he too has been under the illusion of tragic heroism. By wanting to find the essence of things outside of time—to understand, at a given instant, the full genius of La Berma, the greatness of the church at Balbec, or the sui generis attraction of Oriane de Guermantes—Marcel has been searching for a single moment to end all his anticipations and anxieties, for an answer to his strivings and dissatisfactions. This is a tragic-heroic position. As a kind of antidote to the vicissitudes of time, Marcel wishes to have it all—or understand it all, or enjoy it all—in one fell swoop, and he is constantly dissatisfied precisely because he is always left with the impression that time—and, more specifically, the future—is hiding or keeping something from him.

Yet Marcel's third and final interpretation of the crucial scene between Phèdre and Hippolyte, by recognizing the inevitability and even the value of loss, ends his tragic relation to time:

But even if [Hippolyte] had not had this indignant reaction [to the first, ambiguous part of Phèdre's confession], Phèdre, feeling happiness within her grasp, might have had the same feeling [as I had] that happiness wasn't worth much. But as soon as she sees that she hasn't reached what she sought, that Hippolyte thinks he has misunderstood her and is trying to apologize, then, just as I had just given my letter back to Françoise, she *wants the refusal to come from him.* (3.459, my emphasis)

For both Marcel and Phèdre, sending the message results in the ultimate absence or flight of the love object. Marcel may claim to believe that by telling Albertine to stay away he will lure her back to his side (3.457, 461), and Phèdre may secretly hope that Hippolyte, openly confronted with her desire, will not reject her, but in both cases the sender of the message undoubtedly understands, if only at a subconscious level, that the message being sent will lead to an irrevocable loss. Moreover, both Marcel and Phèdre *as Marcel interprets her here* have need of that loss: the narrator makes almost explicit the fact that Marcel's reason for sending the letter is not only his wish to lure Albertine back to his side, but also his need to be rejected by her; like Phèdre in his reading of her, he *wants the refusal to come from the other.*

But why this seeking out of loss? What moves Marcel out of the domain of tragedy here is the text's understanding—which does not emerge explicitly but rather is expressed by the triple intertext—of the role of time in its own literary "type." The essence of that "type," the peculiar novelistic undertaking that is *A la recherche du temps perdu,* is to be found neither in a single moment (lyric) nor in the attempt to stop or stabilize the passage of time (tragedy), but rather in the relation between moments. The passage of time challenges both of the "foreign" types that are put into play in this intertext: lyric, which cannot be temporalized, and tragedy, which has a temporal dimension but struggles against time through the hero's attempt to establish an unchanging position. But Proust's own "type," rather than recapturing or even eternalizing a single moment or series of moments, here shows an understanding that the relation between moments involves recognizing the necessity of death—or of loss as its analogue—as the precondition of the establishment of value.

The recognition of the value of absence and loss is, as we saw in our discussion of Swann, profoundly Pentateuchal:

There are in our soul things to which we don't know how much we are attached. Either, if we live without them, it is because we put off from day to day, from fear of failure or of suffering, entering into their possession. . . . Or, if the thing is in our possession, we believe that it is a burden to us, that we would gladly get rid of it. (3.458)

The things that are most important to us are the very things that we both *need* to possess and *cannot* possess; were Albertine to come back to Marcel, he would once again wish her absent (3.458), and yet it is only insofar as she might escape from him that he wishes to possess her. That Marcel's analysis of a Phèdre who desires Hippolyte only so long as she cannot possess him is Pentateuchal is borne out by a comment that follows his analysis of the confession scene:

> At least that is how, by minimizing all the "Jansenist" scruples, as Bergotte would have put it, that Racine gave Phèdre to make her seem less guilty, I thought of this scene, a kind of prophecy of the amorous episodes of my own existence. (3.460)

When one removes Phèdre's "Jansenist" scruples one is left with an essentially Pentateuchal Phèdre: in Marcel's non-Jansenist analysis it is because Hippolyte and Albertine *cannot* be possessed that they take on and retain their value. It is because no moment is full, because he cannot feel satisfied in the present, that Marcel ultimately places value in the passage of time. Phèdre's relation to Hippolyte is a "prophecy" of Marcel's relation to Albertine; it is not a type implicitly leading to an antitype, but simply a pattern of loss, desire to regain, and realization of the fundamental value of loss.

But if Proust's novel situates value in the passage of time and the endless process of loss that it brings, what does this mean in terms of the principle of typology that set our reading into motion? If Marcel's decision to send Albertine away and not marry her is the key to his status as a New Testament antitype to Swann's type, how can the literary type of the novel, the writing of which is precisely what makes him go beyond his "Judaic" precursor, be a type that valorizes human temporality and loss rather than redemption?

We may find the solution to this seeming paradox if we allow the text's literary typology to provide an alternate model to Christian typology. When the text defines its literary type in opposition to lyric and tragedy, it does so not as an act of pure rejection, but as a process of differentiation that uses the similarity of issues raised by these three different types—and more specifically, their relation to temporality—in order to understand its own characteristics. Analogously, although the loss of Albertine is the moment that marks Marcel's ultimate difference from Swann (even if we do not yet understand the full extent of that difference), it is also, simultaneously, inextricably, a Pentateuchal moment. If there is a New Testament antitype here insofar as Marcel is rejecting posterity, there is also a Pentateuchal type, for the text recognizes the rejection of Albertine and of posterity not only as a potential source of (Christian) salvation, but also as a loss, and as a source of value-through-loss. Instead of an antitype that takes precedence over a type, we find two types interacting with each other, just as Swann's way and the Guermantes way are ultimately shown to intersect (3.692). In recognizing his need for Albertine's absence Marcel may be paving the way for the artistic epiphanies of *Le Temps retrouvé* that have been emphasized by critics; nonetheless, as a literary (more than a theological) type, this is not only a text of redemption, but also a text of loss.

Thus when Proust uses Racine—the very Racine who in the Mallarmé intertext provides an articulation between tragedy and the timelessness of Christian lyric—as an articulation between tragedy and the novel, it is largely through an Old Testament structure, the recognition of the value of temporality and loss. Moreover, virtually the only two Racine plays other than *Phèdre* to which Proust alludes in the *Recherche* are Racine's two Old Testament plays, *Esther* and *Athalie*.[32] Albertine's absence may be necessary as a Christian antitype to Swann's marriage to Odette, but rather than simply proclaiming her absence (or any absence) as a source of redemption and salvation through the relegation of temporality, the text mourns her loss, and the whole of human loss, all the while identifying loss as one of its own prerequisites: Marcel's refusal to call Albertine back is followed almost immediately by her death.

At this crucial triple–crossroads Proust's text vacillates among several literary types, and perhaps several theological types as well, and when, after Marcel's analysis of Racine (via Mallarmé) and his transmission of Mallarmé (via Racine), the text sends the two other literary types on their way, it is not claiming the superiority of its own type over others, but, on the contrary, expressing the desire and the temptation of other types. Proust's initial plan for the *Recherche*, a series of poetic tableaux only loosely connected into any kind of *histoire*, was essentially lyrical, and we have seen that one of the reasons for Marcel's obsession with *Phèdre* is his own tragic impulse. Might we then suggest that the intersection of Proust's text and these two other textual types does not lead to the establishment of his own text as an "antitype"—that is, a progression over other types—but rather is an expression of the paths toward which his own type periodically leads and from which it wistfully distinguishes itself? If this is true, then the saving grace (*salut*) of intertextuality is that texts look at other texts not with a view toward saving them but with a greeting (*salut*) that simply acknowledges their types, and sends them on their way—be it Swann's, or the Guermantes's, or any other way.

The starting point of this "tryptext" was a letter from Marcel to Albertine, and I would like to conclude with one final Racine intertext in Proust's novel, one that is also epistolary. In *A l'ombre des jeunes filles en fleurs*, Albertine hears of two examination topics on Racine:

One was: "Sophocles writes to Racine from the underworld to console him for the failure of *Athalie*"; the other: "Imagine that after the first performance of *Esther*, Madame de Sévigné writes to Madame de La Fayette to tell her how much she regretted her absence." (1.911)

Proust's narrator opines that the letter from Sophocles to Racine is the more difficult of the two examination topics given—not least, perhaps, because it is a letter from the past to the future. But both Sophocles and Madame de Sévigné are at least given the advantage of writing to a literary figure who is their own type, Sophocles to another tragedian and Madame de Sévigné to another master of classical prose (although it is, appropriately, Madame de Sévigné, the expert letter-writer, who holds the pen here). What then might be the difficulties of a letter from Proust to Racine or to Mallarmé, the novelist corresponding with a tragedian or a lyric poet?

Perhaps Proust's letter to Mallarmé and Racine—or rather "around" Mallarmé and Racine, around the obstacles as well as the temptations that their texts pose—is the very text that has formed the basis of this chapter, Marcel's letter to Albertine, via *Phèdre*. And if the fatuous test essay giving the text of the letter from Sophocles to Racine (1.912) shows us the dangers of trying to elaborate the terms of such a text too precisely, let us rather follow the model of Mallarmé, whose own texts form an inextricable part of Proust's letter to Racine, and speculate that the parting message of one *literary* (and not theological) type to another might be nothing more than *salut*.

PART II

REPRESENTATION OF TIME AND MOVEMENT

Chapter 3

PROUST, BERGSON, AND ZENO, OR,

HOW NOT TO REACH ONE'S END

BERGSON AND ZENO

LONG BEFORE the publication of *A la recherche du temps perdu* was complete, critics began to notice a number of points of contact between Proust's masterpiece and the work of the philosopher Henri Bergson. In fact, it would hardly be an exaggeration to say that in the three-quarters of a century since *Du côté de chez Swann* came out, critics have rarely stopped noticing these points of contact. What I will undertake in this chapter is neither an overview of this already long and complex critical debate nor a synthesis of the different positions that have constituted it.[1] Rather, I would like to approach this relation between Proust and Bergson through the intermediary of the pre-Socratic philosopher Zeno of Elea. Zeno is mainly remembered today as the author of four famous paradoxes, all dealing with movement. The questions he raised have undergone a sort of renaissance of interest dating back to the 1880s, a time when both Proust and Bergson were young men.[2] Bergson makes frequent and prominent reference to Zeno and his theories, and while Proust's novel never actually mentions Zeno, its approach to time and change often seems an illustration— albeit an unexpected and original one—of Zeno's paradoxes.

Of the four paradoxes attributed to Zeno, the two most important for our purposes are the paradox of Achilles and the tortoise and the paradox of the arrow. They are stated by Bergson in this way:

> Achilles . . . will never catch up with the tortoise he is running after, because when he arrives at the point from which the tortoise began, the tortoise will have had time to walk further, and so on, indefinitely.[3]

> What can we say about the arrow in flight? At each instant, Zeno says, it is motionless, since it would have time to move, that is, to occupy at least two successive positions, only if it were accorded at least two instants. At any given moment, it is thus at rest at a given point. Motionless at each point of its path, it is motionless the entire time that it is moving.[4]

In the context of the pre-Socratic dispute over the nature of the universe, with some parties claiming that the cosmos is in constant flux and others that it is immutable,[5] Zeno's paradoxes seem to take the latter position, to deny the reality of movement and to suggest that the universe is static and unchanging. But Bergson, considering Zeno's paradoxes in a post-Kantian context, interprets them as being indicative of the human being's inability to *comprehend* change and movement by means of reason or intelligence:

> In [Bergson's] opinion, the aim of Zeno's paradoxes is not at all to challenge the reality of Movement, nor the reality of the Continuous. In fact the paradoxes are a much more destructive force than that. They attack human Intelligence; not only its object (as Kant was to do), but its function. For they are not at all about questioning the existence of Movement, which no one contests (not even Kant). What they are about is whether human intelligence can *grasp* movement. In this area intelligence shows itself to be woefully inadequate: far from being able to grasp movement, it cannot even circumscribe it. So that the aim of Zeno's arguments—let us be clear about this—is not of a "critical" order (in the Kantian sense of the term); it is of an epistemological order. What is being questioned is the workings of intelligence (*episteme*).[6]

Zeno's paradoxes deal with the difficulty of conceptualizing and quantifying motion; not the space or distance covered, but motion itself. This underlying issue of all four of Zeno's paradoxes is summarized by Bergson in this way:

> All of them imply a confusion between movement and distance covered, or at least the conviction that movement can be treated just like space, that it can be divided up without any account being made of its articulations.[7]

Bergson uses his analysis of Zeno's paradoxes as a springboard for a critique of a deep-seated tendency of Western philosophy. At a very early stage in the development of philosophy, Bergson claims, a *parti pris* was established in favor of systematic views of reality. In order to deal with understandable, quantifiable units, philosophers turned their backs on the paradox common to all of Zeno's problems: undoubtedly led by Aristotle, they began to think about the world in terms of stable, unchanging categories and to leave aside the problems entailed in trying to understand the true nature of movement.

Thus, as Bergson claims,

> Metaphysics dates back to the day Zeno of Elea pointed out the contradictions inherent to movement and change, or at least to the way our intelligence represents them. . . . Metaphysics was thus led to search for the reality of things in a realm superior to temporality, beyond what moves and changes; in short outside of what our senses and our consciousness perceive. From that time on metaphysics could be nothing but a more or less artificial arrangement of concepts, a hypothetical construction. It claimed to go be-

yond experience; in reality it did nothing more than replace full, moving experience capable of an ever-growing depth . . . with a fixed, dried up, empty extract, a system of general abstract ideas.[8]

Bergson claims that in attempting to understand change and movement in terms of "general abstract ideas" readily graspable by the intelligence, philosophers have imposed on the domain of change and temporality categories that are entirely inappropriate to it. What Zeno's paradoxes tell us is that change and movement are sui generis and thus escape all attempts at schematization. Change and temporality are not reducible to either the general or the abstract: they are utterly particular.

I would like to suggest that this conclusion Bergson reaches in his interpretation of Zeno's paradoxes can be extremely fruitful to the reader of Proust's monumental novel of time and temporality. There would undoubtedly be many ways to study the *Recherche* in terms of either the problem of the limits of knowledge[9] or that of the nature of temporality.[10] What I will do here is bring these two issues together, as Bergson's analysis of Zeno does. Some of the questions that result from this conjunction are these: What is the nature of our perception of temporal movement? Is knowledge of diachronic change possible? Is knowledge of temporal movement knowledge of the general or that of the particular? And does Proust's novel ultimately take a Zenonian or an anti-Zenonian position? Let us now approach Proust's novel with these questions in mind.

Swann, the Zenonian Man

"Un Amour de Swann" ("Swann in Love"), which occupies roughly the second half of *Du côté de chez Swann,* is perhaps the single section in the entire cycle of novels in which the question of gradual, continuous change is most acutely (even though not explicitly) posed. Certainly the famous scene of the matinée Guermantes that closes *Le Temps retrouvé* largely consists of Marcel's observations of a series of shocking changes in those around him, but that scene deals with discontinuous change: what is depicted is not the process of change but rather the revelation of the distressingly different states in which Marcel finds people whom he has not seen for many years. By contrast, one of the central issues of "Un Amour de Swann" is the very process by which Swann falls in love with Odette de Crécy, the gradual evolution of the relationship from indifference to attachment, jealousy, and mad possessiveness, with a subsequent return to indifference, and finally, long after the time period of the narrative is over, marriage.

Although "Un Amour de Swann" arouses our interest in the question of change, and although it arguably provides the smoothest, most continuous narrative of Proust's entire work, this does not mean that its depiction of the continuous process of falling in love is adequate. Not only is the reader not fully aware of when or how or even why Swann falls in love with Odette, but Swann himself appears to be unaware of it; it escapes his perception and understanding as much as ours.

In fact Swann can be seen as the archetypal Zenonian man:

> He had in his soul the lack of suppleness that certain beings have in their bodies, people who at the instant of avoiding a shock, of moving a flame away from their clothing, or of carrying out some other urgent movement, take their time, start out staying for a second in the situation in which they found themselves before and in which they might find their point of support, their momentum [*élan*].[11]

This description of Swann is reminiscent of the paradox underlined and criticized by Bergson: Swann is one of those people who look for the source of their movement, their *élan*, in a static position or "situation." When Bergson says that "we reason about movement as if it were composed of immobilities,"[12] he might be speaking about Swann's attempts to initiate movement.

Indeed, when, on the fateful evening that Swann misses Odette at the Verdurins', then realizes how important she has become to him (without, of course, knowing exactly when or how) and goes chasing after her, he becomes a kind of Achilles running after a tortoise, an illustration of the Proustian maxim that a person whom we love "makes our life into a kind of moving expanse [*étendue émouvante*] in which he will be closer or farther from us" (1.236). One wonders whether Swann will ever catch up with his goal, partly because it is his footman, rather than he himself, who is doing the moving, but even more importantly because of his own curious emotional makeup:

> The footman came back, but when he came to a stop next to Swann, the latter did not say, "Did you find the lady?" but rather, "Remind me to order some wood tomorrow, I think the woodpile is getting low." . . . And probably, if the footman had interrupted him to say, "I have found the lady," he would have responded, "Oh yes, that's right, that errand that I asked you to run [*la course que je vous ai donnée*, literally "the run that I gave you"], goodness, I didn't think you'd find her," and he would have gone on talking about woodpiles to hide the emotion he had felt and *to give himself the time he needed to break relations with his uneasiness and to give himself over to happiness*. (1.229–30, my emphasis)

Swann himself does not at first run after Odette, but rather "gives the run" to his footman. Moreover, even if the footman had found Odette, Swann's affliction, his difficult relation to change and movement that we might call "zenonitis," would have prevented him from assimilating the emotional change that catching her should have brought about. Once again, Swann cannot simply move from one point or from one state to another (in this case, from "uneasiness" to "happiness") in the sort of smooth, indivisible sweep that Bergson claims characterizes movement. Instead he must "break" with the old state and then catch up with the new one.

Swann does finally take to his heels to run after Odette, but it is not for this reason that he finds her. Rather than catching up with the object of his affection, he bumps into her: "He pushed on to the Maison Dorée, went into Tortoni's twice, and had just come out of the Café Anglais without finding her there, walking with great strides and a worn look about him, . . . when he bumped into a person who was moving in the opposite direction: it was Odette. . . ." (1.231). We can only be thankful that Swann and Odette ultimately move in opposite directions, for in spite of his "great strides" Swann is a hopeless pursuer. Even when he "catches" Odette, when, in the carriage, he is about to kiss her for the first time, his "zenonitis" persists:

> Swann was the one who, before she let her face fall, as if in spite of herself, onto his lips, held it an instant, at some distance from himself, in his two hands. He had wished to give his thought the time to catch up [*laisser à sa pensée le temps d'accourir*], to recognize the dream that it had cherished for so long and to be present at the execution of that dream. (1.233)

This passage seems like an illustration of Bergson's title, *La Pensée et le mouvant*; it is about Swann's need to have his thought "catch up with" or run after (*accourir*) the changes in his situation. Just as he has difficulties catching up with Odette, his thought has problems following the movements that are taking place in his life.

GENERIC KNOWLEDGE

The question then becomes this: Why doesn't Swann know how to move? Why is his movement apparently reducible to a series of states—precisely what Bergson says movement should not be reducible to?

Let us first recall that according to Bergson the error of post-Zenonian metaphysics lies in replacing "full, moving experience" with "a fixed, dried up, empty extract, a system of general abstract ideas."

This sterility of the general, its inability to account for the infinite potential of the particular, is related to the all-important concept of genres in Proust's novel.

The term "genre" punctuates Swann's entire adventure with Odette, his initiation into the process of falling in love through time, for as the text takes great pains to emphasize, Odette, unlike all of Swann's previous partners, is *not* his genre:

> But while every one of these relationships, or rather flings, had been the realization—more or less complete—of a dream sprung from the glimpse of a face or a figure that Swann had spontaneously, without any effort, found charming, by contrast when one day at the theater he was introduced to Odette de Crécy by one of his old friends, . . . Swann had found her certainly not lacking in beauty, but of a type [*genre*] of beauty that left him indifferent. (1.195)

> To think that I've wasted years of my life, that I've wished for death, that I've experienced my greatest love, for a woman whom I didn't like, who wasn't my type [*qui n'était pas mon genre*]! (1.382)

Both at the beginning and at the end of "Un Amour de Swann," we are pointedly informed that Odette is not Swann's genre. What is the importance of this framing of "Un Amour de Swann" by a term that, as Swann points out, is apparently *not* operative in his love for Odette?

In fact Swann's evolving relationship with Odette is at least implictly measured against a norm of virtually all social relations in Proust's universe, a norm based on genres. It is true that Swann's taste in women is not limited to a conventionally definable social class or milieu, but his reliance upon genre in his amorous exchanges is profoundly consonant with the basic operation of Proustian society, in which the genre is a fundamental identifying unit of social value and position.

Proust's social world is divided into a certain number of homogeneous groups, *petits clans* or *petits noyaux* if one follows the terminology of the monstrous Madame Verdurin, *coteries* in the vocabulary of Swann and the Guermantes. The time period in which the work is set saw a great deal of social mobility in France—Swann himself is a striking example of the possibilities of *arrivisme* under the Third Republic—and within the novel there is certainly a good amount of switching *coteries* and long-term evolution of individual *clans*, as the brilliant matinée of the Princesse de Guermantes (ex–Madame Verdurin) in *Le Temps retrouvé* demonstrates. But although there are some possibilities of exchange between these social units, each unit, whatever its position on the social scale, has its own genre. The principal characteristic of a *cote-rie* is suggested by the term "social set"; its genre is set, unchanging:

> To be a part of the "little core" [*petit noyau*], the "little group," the "little clan" of the Verdurins, one condition was sufficient but it was necessary: one had to adhere tacitly to a Credo that was partly composed of the belief that the young pianist who was under Madame Verdurin's wing that year and about whom she said, "It should be illegal to know how to play Wagner that well!" left both Planté and Rubinstein "in the mud" and that Doctor Cottard had a better diagnostic eye than Potain. Any "new recruit" who could not be convinced by the Verdurins that the *soirées* of people who did not frequent their house were dull as ditchwater found himself instantly excluded. (1.188)

It matters little what the particulars of the Credo are—indeed, like the vicissitudes of fashion, they change from season to season. What does matter is that the social set remain a homogeneous group, as identical to itself as it is different from others.[13] When Swann, in the course of his first evening with the *petit clan*, makes several "particular remarks" [*remarques particulières*] about the beauty of Vinteuil's sonata, Madame Verdurin sets him straight: "No one wastes time splitting hairs here, it's just not the style [*genre*] of the house" (1.213). And what ultimately expels him is that he feels for Odette "an affection that was too particular and about which he had failed to confide regularly in Madame Verdurin" (1.249).

Genres, then, like habits, are profoundly conservative in nature. They establish unchanging patterns of thought and action and resist change and movement. But Proust's novel repeatedly questions the authenticity of genres by revealing them as meaningless social categories that prevent rather than allow knowledge. The Duchesse de Guermantes is exemplary when she says she will not pay a call on the Iénas, some unfashionable friends of her husband's, because, as she says, "I don't know them" [*je ne les connais pas*]:

> "I would rush over to their house with Basin, I would go see them even in the midst of their sphinxes and their copperware if I knew them, but . . . I don't know them! I was always told when I was a girl that it was impolite to visit people one didn't know," she said in a childish tone of voice. "So I do what I've been taught." (1.339)

In saying that these people are not her genre and that she therefore does not want to visit them, Oriane is implicitly making two opposing statements. She is saying both that she does not know them socially, that is, has not met them, and that she does know their genre well enough to know that she does not want to know them. Knowing their genre is a way of knowing them at a distance, from the outside, and it saves her the trouble of knowing them in any other way. Following Gilles Deleuze, we might consider the genre to be a kind of *signe mondain* or social sign of knowledge that, like all social signs, "takes the place of action and thought" rather than simply representing them.[14] When Oriane says that she will not go to see her husband's friends because she does not know them, she is actually reversing cause and effect: she does not know them *because* she will not go to see them. Her statement, "I don't know them," could be applied to virtually anyone, whether within her *coterie* or outside of it: at the same time as she seems to know practically everyone by genre, she knows no one by anything else. Like the bourgeois snob Legrandin, she could truthfully say, "je connais tout le monde et je ne connais personne"; "I know everyone and I know no one" (1.131).

Thus the aristocratic Comte de Forcheville has a certain fascination when he penetrates the Verdurins' *petit clan* simply because he has a different genre from the rest of the *fidèles*:

> From the very beginning of the meal, . . . the doctor . . . had not stopped observing him [Forcheville], for he was very curious to find out what the kind of person he called a *"de"* [i.e., a titled aristocrat] was like. (1.251)

Doctor Cottard observes the Comte de Forcheville, a man with a title and thus a *de* in front of his name, as he might examine a specimen of an unknown species or genus. The "particle" in front of the Comte's name gives rise to a meaningful wordplay when the Verdurins discuss the relative merits of Swann and the Comte after their guests have departed:

> "Did you notice how Swann laughed in a ridiculous way when we spoke about Madame La Trémoïlle?"
>
> She [Madame Verdurin] had noticed that in front of that name Swann and Forcheville had left out the particle [*supprimé la particule*, i.e., left out the word *de*] several times. Having no doubt that this was to show that they were not intimidated by titles, she wished to imitate their pride, but had not quite figured out the grammatical form it took. . . .
>
> And Monsieur Verdurin answered her: ". . . Swann wants to rub our noses in his society connections, . . . but at least the other one has his title; he's still the Comte de Forcheville," he added delicately, as if he knew all about the history of that earldom and were minutely weighing its particular value [*la valeur particulière*]. (1.265)

"La valeur particulière" has two opposing meanings here. Monsieur Verdurin is purportedly judging the value of the Comte de Forcheville as a unique, discrete individual, what the French might call *un particulier*,

or private citizen. But actually he is judging him purely as a general type: his *valeur particulière* to Monsieur Verdurin is nothing more than the value of his *particule*, the general category of titled aristocrat—what Cottard would call his *de*—into which he falls.

"Une femme(,) qui n'était pas mon genre"

If we now return to Swann's love for a woman who is not his genre, we can see that it is played out against the background of a society in which social interactions—both Swann's own past love affairs and relations in the world at large—function by genres. Before Swann meets Odette, his love life consists of a movement from one woman who is his genre to the next; it has a "permanent character and identical goals" (1.193). For Swann, then, even though he changes women constantly, operating by types or genres is a way of avoiding any profound change, or at least of limiting his perception of temporality to a series of essentially unchanging states. At any given moment Swann is infatuated with a given woman, but since his relations never develop through time, the links between those states—the very links that might be assumed to constitute movement itself—are merely empty transitions. Swann's love life is thus profoundly affected by his "zenonitis." It may be schematized into a series of static points—separated from one another by transitions unimportant in themselves—which are in no way integrated into a movement.

Indeed, the fact that Odette is not Swann's genre makes it difficult for him to remember her through time, for never before have his loves had a temporal component:

> Odette de Crécy came back to see Swann again, then began to visit him more frequently; and undoubtedly each of her visits renewed the disappointment he felt at seeing a face whose particular features he had somewhat forgotten in the interval [*ce visage dont il avait un peu oublié les particularités dans l'intervalle*] . . . ; he felt sorry, as she chatted with him, that the great beauty that she had was not the type [*genre*] of beauty he would have spontaneously preferred. (1.197)

The particularities of Odette's face are difficult for Swann to remember not only because she is not his genre, but also because he is not used to dealing with anything other than genres; the particular is not a part of "Swann's way" of thinking and perceiving. The "intervals" between Odette's visits are also the intervals between Swann's genre as a general principle of love (or attraction) and Odette's particular features, which do not match that genre.

In Bergson's terms, what Swann has given up in transcending the genre as an artificial unit of conceptualization is a simple (not to say simplistic) way of dealing with time and change: "[General concepts must] fill in the intervals [*combler les intervalles*] between the givens of the senses or of consciousness and hence unify and systematize our knowledge of things."[15] To "fill in the intervals" between Swann's perception of the "particularities" of Odette's face on a given visit and his perception of them on the next visit is to have a general concept of Odette. But since she is not his genre, that is exactly what he does not have. It is perhaps for this reason that Swann also has trouble seeing the continuity of Odette's figure:

> As for her body, which was wonderfully well built, it was difficult to perceive its continuity, . . . for the bodice of her dress, protruding as if to cover an imaginary belly and then coming briskly to a point [*pointe*] while the double skirts started to balloon up from underneath, made the woman look as if she were made up of different pieces that fit together badly. (1.197)

Odette's dress, with its ample bodice and wide skirts tapering sharply to a tiny waist that seems almost inexistent ("pointe"), gives her the shape of a human hourglass, the hourglass being an early attempt to measure the passage of time rather than understand its true nature, its incommensurability, as Bergson or Zeno might point out. Swann's difficulty in "perceiving the continuity" of Odette's body is a metaphor for his difficulty in gaining any coherent knowledge of her across time, in seizing her in her particularity without the aid of a genre.

It is because time does not allow Swann to know Odette that it does allow him—almost force him—to fall in love with her. The birth of Swann's love for Odette as a particular woman rather than a general type is announced by the phrase *faire catleya*, Swann's and Odette's "particular way of saying 'to make love'" (1.234). Whereas Swann considers "possessing the most different women always the same and known ahead of time" so long as he possesses only their genre, *faire catleya* is specific to this relationship: "perhaps it didn't mean exactly the same thing as its synonyms" (1.234).

Emblematic of Odette's particularization in Swann's eyes is a ritual that is more innocent than *faire catleya* but equally crucial to their relationship, the ritual of making tea:

> Odette made Swann "his" tea, asked him: "Lemon or cream?" and as he answered "cream," laughingly said to him: "A cloud!" And as he found it good: "You see that I know what you like." Indeed this tea had seemed like something precious to Swann, as it had to Odette, and . . . when he had left her at seven o'clock to go home and get dressed, during the entire trip home

in his carriage, hardly able to contain the joy that the afternoon had caused him, he said to himself over and over: "How nice it would be to have a lovely person like that whom one could visit in order to get that rarity, good tea" [*cette chose si rare, du bon thé*]. (1.221–22)

The tea Odette makes for Swann is the embodiment of her particular value—and of the value of the particular—for him. In the context of "Un Amour de Swann," which consists largely of a narration of how small, even rather petty events take on tremendous importance, it would hardly be frivolous to say that knowing how another person takes his tea is a metaphor for being thoroughly familiar with his ways. It is the sort of homey and intimate detail that ex-lovers and divorced couples remember about each other after years of separation. It is not just the precise quantity of cream that makes this particular cup of tea of Swann's into "his" tea—otherwise *du bon thé* would presumably not be *cette chose si rare*—but all of the particulars of the ritual, including Odette's way of calling the splash of cream she tips in "a cloud." *Un nuage* is no more generalizable to a predictable amount of cream than *faire catleya* is generalizable to *faire l'amour*.

Intellectually Swann fully realizes that this value that Odette comes to have for him is not reducible to any communicable, general principle:

He quite felt that his love was something that did not correspond to anything external or affirmable by anyone other than himself; he realized that Odette's qualities did not justify his placing so high a value on the moments he spent by her side. And often, when positive intelligence alone got the better of Swann, he wished to put an end to his sacrificing of so many intellectual and social interests to this imaginary pleasure. (1.236)

Odette resists attempts at placing an abstract value upon her. Although Madame Verdurin applies several rather vague terms to her ("un amour," 1.188; "une petite perfection," 191), she must concede her husband's claim that Odette "is neither a virtue nor an intelligence" (1.228).

But this difficulty of generalizing Odette is not purely benign, for once the inadequacy of genres is recognized, it leaves behind an utterly destabilized world, a world in which Swann experiences the infinite potential of the particular as a kind of psychological overload. When the very notion of genres has collapsed, Swann falls into a veritable mania of the particular, as he becomes obsessed by Odette's every moment and by the growing need to be master of all of her particular relations—real or potential—with others. And what he then discovers is that he cannot count on anything, not even on his own memories of

Odette. When Swann finds out that Odette has had a recent sexual encounter with another woman on the island of the Bois de Boulogne, this is his reaction:

> Never had he assumed that it was such a recent thing, hidden from his eyes ... not in a past he had not known, but in evenings he remembered so well, evenings that he had spent with Odette, which he had thought he knew so well...; in their midst, suddenly, gaped that hollow opening [*se creusait cette ouverture béante*], the moment in the *île du Bois*. (1.366)

Instead of calming his jealousy as he says it will ("C'est si calmant de se représenter les choses," 1.365), Odette's report of the details of her infidelity feeds Swann's desire to divide and subdivide her time into fully accountable moments. A single moment in Odette's life is transformed into an endless, unfilled space ("ouverture béante"), a cosmos of possibilities; it leads to a kind of Pascalian collapse, by which the infinitely small (moment) becomes in Swann's mind like an entire new universe containing yet another infinity of "concealing moments" ("moments receleurs," 1.371) or submoments to analyze. Thus even Odette's confessions "functioned for Swann like points of departure leading to new doubts rather than putting an end [*un terme*] to old ones" (1.370).

Swann's attempt to go beyond genres in his love for Odette, far from solving Zeno's paradoxes, aggravates his own "zenonitis." What he discovers is that a love anchored in the particular does not circumvent the problem of continuity posed by Zeno's division of time into discrete moments, but rather is ultimately revealed to be so acutely unstable—since nothing, not even a particular moment, can be known in its entirety—that it offers a feeling of profound discontinuity:

> What we believe to be our love, our jealousy, is not a single, continuous, indivisible passion. Rather they are composed of an infinity of successive loves, of different jealousies that are ephemeral but that because of their uninterrupted multitude give an impression of continuity, the illusion of unity. (1.372)

Swann has known two kinds of love: generic love and particular love. Generic love, which is based on a single principle, does not evolve through time. Particular love, by contrast, develops through time but has no unifying principle; it is an aggregation of particular moments. Swann's love for Odette may create an "impression of continuity" and an "illusion of unity," but so long as it is love of the particular, the impression and the illusion are false.

But this is not the end of Swann's relationship with Odette. What finally happens when Swann decides to marry Odette and formalize their relationship is that he relegates his search for the particular, or at least implicitly admits that it is a failure, and marries an Odette who, *precisely because she is not understandable*, must be made generalizable, that is, associable (artificially) with an abstract principle. While good tea or *"bon thé"* made Swann fall in love with Odette as a particular woman, what makes him marry her is a general concept, her kindness or *"bonté"*:

> She was there, often tired, her face momentarily emptied of her feverish and joyful preoccupation with those unknown things that made Swann suffer; she parted [*écartait*] her hair with her hands; her forehead and her face seemed broader; then, suddenly, some simple human thought, some kind sentiment of the sort that exists in all creatures, when in a moment of rest or withdrawal they are left to their own devices, sprang from her eyes like a yellow ray. And instantly her whole face lit up like a gray countryside covered with clouds that suddenly part, for its transfiguration, at sunset. . . . As rare as they became, these moments were not wasted. Through memory Swann linked together the fragments, abolished the intervals [*abolissait les intervalles*], and cast, as in gold, an Odette of kindness [*une Odette de bonté*] and of calm for whom he later made . . . sacrifices that the other Odette would not have inspired. (1.314)

Une Odette de bon thé and *une Odette de bonté*: these are the two Odettes that represent, respectively, the particular and the general for Swann. Those "unknown things that made Swann suffer" and that preoccupy Odette are exactly the sorts of particular memories and plans that drive him to distraction largely because he comes to feel he can never exhaust them, never know all there is to know about Odette. But when on rare occasions her face is emptied of all particularity, she becomes simply a human being, capable of kindness and compassion as any human being is.

It is this "general" Odette, a sort of generic human being, whom Swann will marry, this being the greatest of his "sacrifices" alluded to here. Just as he could not remember the particularities of Odette's face "in the interval" between their visits because he had no general principle that he could attach to her, he now gives her a definitive unity by "abolishing the intervals" between these rare moments in which she reaches the stature of the general and "casting" Odette in the mold of an abstract principle: "bonté." To move from "bon thé" to "bonté" requires nothing more than to "abolish the interval" between the two syllables—that is, to incorporate the suffix of abstraction "-té" to one of Odette's qualities—for in so doing one also abolishes the intervals separating the different moments of Odette's existence. It is true that this does not make Odette into a purely good woman, any more than choosing to cast her in the mold of *cruauté*, for example, would make her unmitigatedly cruel. But it does allow Swann to stabilize Odette through an attachment to the general and the abstract in a way that no relation to the particular ever could.

The conflict between particular and general is reinforced here by the simile of the clouds. Odette parting her hair to let her unwonted expression of kindness ("bonté") shine through is compared to a gray countryside over which the clouds part at sunset. But let us recall that what gives her such success as a maker of good tea ("bon thé") is that she knows how to pour "a cloud" of cream. The cloud of cream, as we saw earlier, is the epitome of the particular; like *faire catleya*, it is an irreplaceable part of a ritual that, without it, might well seem commonplace and nondescript. But it is exactly this particularization of Odette that must be "parted" (*écarté*) from her before Swann can stabilize his relationship with her.

By marrying the "Odette de bonté" rather than the "Odette de bon thé," Swann is not claiming to have solved Zeno's paradoxes, but tacitly conceding defeat at their hands. He is indicating that he will never know Odette as a particular woman, will never grasp her as a being infinitely capable of change and thus impossible to quantify. His revolt against the general and ultimate return to it give the final phrase of "Un Amour de Swann" a tremendous ambiguity, an ambiguity that sums up much of the power of this peculiar narrative: "To think that I've wasted years of my life, that I've wished for death, that I've experienced my greatest love, for a woman whom I didn't like, who wasn't my type [*une femme qui ne me plaisait pas, qui n'était pas mon genre*]!" (1.382). Perhaps Swann does indeed experience his greatest love for a woman who is not his genre. But that is not the woman he marries. The woman he marries is not exactly his genre, either, but she is the generically kind Odette, the Odette who could be essentially any woman, just as Molly recalls at the end of Joyce's *Ulysses* that she decided to marry Bloom as she might have decided to marry any man: "and I thought well as well him as another."[16]

The ambiguous syntax of Swann's last sentence tells us of this final victory of the generic over the particular. The phrases "qui ne me plaisait pas" and "qui n'était pas mon genre" are more or less synonymous. Now if we wish to leave aside the first of the two phrases and consider the syntax of only the second phrase, the sentence can be punctuated in two different ways:

une femme qui n'était pas mon genre!

une femme, qui n'était pas mon genre!

In other words, the comma preceding "qui n'était pas mon genre," which serves the purpose of separating the two apposed synonymous phrases from each other, can also (but need not) serve the function of separating "une femme" from "qui n'était pas mon genre." This may seem fastidious, but there is in fact a radical difference in meaning between the clauses "a woman who was not my type [*genre*]" and "a woman, [that is, a person] who was not my gender [*genre*]." In the first case the noun "woman" is delimited by what follows: we are dealing not with just any woman, but with a woman who is not "my type." In the second case what we have is a wonderfully tautological phrase: given the fact that the "I" here is a man, a woman is by definition "someone who is not my gender."

Odette corresponds to both these meanings. It is true that she is not Swann's type, and it is as such, as a particular woman, that he falls in love with her. But it is also true that she is not his gender, that she is a woman like all other women. And it is with this generic woman—a woman he will never really come to know in spite of their many years together—that Swann will choose to spend the rest of his life.

"Une femme dans André(e)"

As we now turn our attention to the protagonist of Proust's novel, we find that he, too, has the possibility of a generic love. The parallels with "Un Amour de Swann" that Marcel's love story offers are, of course, numerous, even including the same distinction between general knowledge of the loved one's infidelity and familiarity with the particulars of her amorous adventures:

> I told myself [Albertine] was probably making ill use of her liberty since her departure, and although that idea had rather saddened me it remained general, showing me nothing particular; because of the indefinite number of possible lovers it allowed me to assume she had while not allowing me to fix on any of them, it dragged my mind along in a sort of perpetual movement that was not exempt from pain, but the pain of which was bearable because of the lack of a concrete image. (3.470)

Just as Swann does not really suffer at the general idea of Odette's infidelity, Marcel is not tormented by jealousy until he is presented with a particular image of Albertine with another woman.

Similarly, Marcel's love moves through essentially the same phases of the general (generic) and the particular as Swann's—Deleuze calls it "the slow individualization of Albertine within the group of girls."[17] And although Marcel never takes the final step of associating Albertine with a general, abstract principle that might mark his realization of the limits of his understanding and perception of her, perhaps his failure to marry Albertine has to do with the conflict between the particular and the general just as much as Swann's marriage to Odette does. In the last letter Marcel sends to Albertine before her death, he announces his plans to marry Albertine's best friend, Andrée:

> Since the fatality of our characters and the misfortunes of life have decided that my little Albertine cannot be my wife, I think I will still have a wife—not so charming as she, but whose nature, in closer conformity to mine, will perhaps allow her to be happier with me—in Andrée [*je crois que j'aurai tout de même une femme . . . dans Andrée*]. (3.469–70)

The name "Andrée," like many of the names of female characters in Proust's novel (Gilberte, Albertine, Léonie, Françoise), is constructed from a masculine name to which a suffix has been added. The masculine name in question, André, comes from the Greek "*aner*," which means "masculine being." To find "une femme . . . dans Andrée" is as tautological as to say that Odette is "une femme, qui n'était pas mon genre"; it is to create a generic woman by adding a feminine suffix to a name meaning "masculine being." From her very first appearance in the novel, Albertine as part of the *petite bande* of girls is potentially substitutable and thus, in a sense, generalizable: if Marcel can replace her with another of the "jeunes filles en fleurs" like Andrée, she is categorizable as a "budding young girl" rather than being a unique, one-of-a-kind individual, Albertine. As soon as Marcel announces his intention of marrying the generic "jeune fille en fleur," Andrée (even assuming his announcement is a ploy), Albertine dies; "j'aurai une femme . . . dans Andrée" are apparently the last words she receives from him.[18]

What this chain of events seems to suggest is something that Swann himself undoubtedly realizes: that accepting the limited possibilities of knowledge of the particular may save one from the feeling of Achillean futility involved in chasing after the particular (or knowledge of it), but that it also means losing the particular. When Swann marries the generic Odette, the particular Odette he loved has already long ago ceased to exist for him, and he understands that she will never again come to life. Marcel's love story simply makes this loss of the particular literal: when at a similar juncture in his own relationship with Albertine Marcel states that he is about to commit himself to a generic marriage to Andrée, his gesture makes him lose Albertine forever.

Involuntary Memory and Genres

But while Marcel is ultimately made to reject genres in the domain of love—since he does not, in fact, marry Andrée—he makes as persistent use of them in other ways as Swann does in love. From the beginning of the novel, Marcel is almost constantly in search of general principles that might hold true through time, indeed, that might free him from the constraints of living in time and accepting its potential for change and movement. It is by contrast to his dissatisfaction with time that the experiences of involuntary memory derive their force, for the premise of these experiences is that they operate by genres and thus are able to supercede the temporal.

In the incident of the madeleine, for example, what the narrator claims to recognize in his analysis of the power of the madeleine is that its taste is "that of the little bit of madeleine that, on Sunday mornings in Combray ..., my Aunt Léonie offered me after soaking it in her tea...." (1.46–47). But of course the taste of one madeleine cannot be precisely that of another madeleine eaten some thirty years earlier (or, for that matter, one moment earlier); what the narrator means here is that the taste is the same "kind" of taste. And this is made explicit in the famous scene of involuntary memory at the matinée Guermantes:

> The napkin I had taken to wipe my mouth had exactly the kind [genre] of stiffness and weight of the one I had had so much trouble drying myself with in front of the window, the first day of my arrival in Balbec, and now, in front of this library of the Guermantes mansion, it spread out ... the plumage of a green and blue ocean like a peacock's tail. (3.869)

Just as the taste of two madeleines soaked in tea at a great interval of time may be the same *in kind*, the texture of two napkins touched many years apart may be of the same genre.

In addition to operating by genres, that is, kinds of sensations, the experience of involuntary memory itself establishes a genre:

> Indeed, the happiness [félicité] that I had just felt [in tripping on the uneven paving stones in the Guermantes's courtyard] was quite the same as the happiness I had felt in eating the madeleine. (3.867)

> [In hearing a spoon struck against a plate], I was invaded by the same kind of happiness [genre de félicité] that the uneven paving stones had given me; [although] the sensations ... were altogether different. (3.868)

The sensations evoked by various experiences of involuntary memory are "altogether different" in their particulars, but the feeling of happiness or *félicité* is of a single genre. Once again the genre thus appears to go beyond temporal difference—the utter particularity and hence unconnectedness of each moment—and to establish immutable, unchanging principles, exactly what Marcel is in search of. The recurrence of a single "kind" of sensation suggests that within the flux and instability of temporal change, some things stay the same.

Is this simply another demonstration of the profoundly conservative nature of genres? Is the text merely implying that even as a middle-aged man, Marcel can at least still have the satisfaction of getting good, old-fashioned madeleines, that the napkins offered by the Guermantes to their guests are as starchy as they used to be in the good old days, and that some things, at least, never seem to change, personal failures and world wars notwithstanding? This is, after all, a text that unashamedly tries to hold on to the past, hence its preoccupation with out-of-date fashions, clothing, and social customs, among other things.

But of course the claims being made here go far beyond the social. What the text seems to be saying is that the persistence of genres in the experience of involuntary memory establishes a permanence of being for a character who otherwise exists in a series of moments with no links between them, a being who, in a vision of temporality remarkably similar to Zeno's, lives time as a series of discontinuities precisely because what he, like Zeno, wants to do is schematize the unschematizable. Proust's narrator himself has, as Georges Poulet puts it, "lost the means to link together the place and the moment in which he is living to all the other places and moments of his earlier existence."[19] And the genres that underlie the experience of involuntary memory appear to remedy that loss.

This is fairly close to what Proust himself explicitly says about the restorative and recuperative possibilities of involuntary memory. But what my entire discussion up to this point has tried to show is that if the problem is understanding temporal change and movement, genres are more a part of the problem than a part of the solution, less a means of acquiring knowledge of temporal movement than a sign of the impossibility of that knowledge. The link between moments briefly established by involuntary memory anticipates the text's discussion of metaphor, which is also a linkage between different elements:

> Truth [*la vérité*] will begin only at the moment when the writer takes two different objects, poses their relation, analogous in the world of art to the unique relation of a causal law in the world of science, and encloses them within the necessary rings of a beautiful style; even, like life itself, when, in bringing together a quality common to two sensations, he emphasizes their common essence by uniting them in order to extract them from the contingencies of time, in a metaphor. (3.889)

Like the links established by involuntary memory, the rings of style and the ties of metaphor bring together two elements that are different; they thus appear to transcend the particularity of those elements through what is essentially a universalizing gesture. Moreover, in all three cases—involuntary memory, style, and metaphor—the victory of the general over the particular is presented as being an initiatory moment. What "will begin" when two different objects are linked by style or metaphor or when two discrete moments are linked by involuntary memory is nothing less momentous than truth: *la vérité*.

But if this *vérité* ushered in by the attainment of a general principle through style or metaphor is related to the truth purportedly understood in the experience of the madeleine, what is its nature? Perhaps, like Odette's *bonté*—another word ending in "-té"—this *vérité* is an abstraction uneasily matched to anything concrete, a generalization that ill fits the particulars to which it is applied. Whatever claims the text may make, it is a *vérité* that never quite makes up for the *loss* of the particular, any more than Swann's marriage to Odette makes up for losing the Odette he used to love. I would like to demonstrate that the narrator's supposed attainment of a general truth is as artificial as Swann's arrival at the "truth" about Odette and her goodness; it is this demonstration that will allow us to draw our final conclusions about Proust's relation to Zeno's paradoxes.

"A PLACE PROLONGED WITHOUT MEASURE IN TIME," OR, ZENO MEETS HIS MATCH

That the madeleine episode abounds in abstract terms ending in "-té" shouldn't surprise us, given its status as a founding moment of general and abstract truth.

> A delicious pleasure had invaded me, isolated, without the notion of its cause. It had immediately made the vicissitudes of life indifferent to me, its disasters inoffensive, its brevity [*brièveté*] illusory. (1.45)

> I put down my cup [*tasse*] and turn toward my mind. I must rely on my mind to find the truth [*vérité*]. (45)

> And I once again begin to wonder about this unknown state, which brings no logical proof but rather evidence—of its felicity, of its reality [*de sa félicité, de sa réalité*]—next to which all else fades. (45)

> And each time the cowardice [*lâcheté*] that makes us turn away from any difficult task, from any important work, advised me to leave all that, to drink my tea [*mon thé*] and simply think about today's worries and tomorrow's desires. (46)

The "vérité" hidden within the experience of the madeleine makes life's "brièveté" illusory. The incident takes place in a state of unprecedented "félicité" and "réalité," and only Marcel's "lâcheté" might stop him from finding out why. Although this is an episode about drinking tea, or "thé," it appears to be less concerned with that humble drink than with grand abstract notions ending in "-té": *vérité, réalité, félicité.*

And yet, just as the value of Swann's image of an "Odette de bonté" can be understood only in relation to the "Odette de bon thé" of which it is the implicit rejection, the proliferation of words ending in "-té" here should not distract us from the importance of Marcel's "thé." The text makes an almost explicit opposition between the great truths sought after here and the brew Marcel is drinking: cowardice tells him to leave aside his search for the truth and to drink his "thé," which, as in Odette's case, becomes a metaphor for the particular—"today's worries and tomorrow's desires," whatever they might be—unattached to any larger or more general scheme of things.

This might lead us to believe that if *veritas* is in *vino*, it is most decidedly not in tea; in the passage quoted above Marcel puts down his "tasse" or cup in order to concentrate on finding the "vérité" he is after. But the last word ending in "-té" in the madeleine episode—and consequently the final abstract term of the long prelude to the *Recherche* that the madeleine episode brings to a close—tells us that if "vérité" is not in "thé," "solidité" is: ". . . all those things that take form and solidity [*solidité*] came out—city and gardens—of my cup of tea [*de ma tasse de thé*]" (1.48). What takes "form and solidity" is precisely the concrete and particular elements of the narration about Combray that immediately follows. And this instantaneous movement toward the particular and away from the enormous questions of truth, reality, and felicity is precisely what is surprising about the relation of the madeleine episode to "Combray." It is true that the narrator makes an important disclaimer about Marcel's noncomprehension of the source of the happiness brought by the madeleine episode at the time it takes place: "I did not yet know and had to put off until much later discovering why this memory made me so happy" (1.47). But the narrator does identify the source of the memory, and the text calls that in itself a kind of truth: "I put down my cup [*tasse*] . . . to find the truth [*vérité*]." What happens to that truth as the main body of the narration begins?

"Vérité" is subsumed by another abstract term, "solidité"—a term that, although itself abstract, marks the limitations of the abstract and the general. The discovery that the reader will make in "Combray" and that will continue to hold good throughout Proust's novel is the utterly unrepresentable nature of each moment, the seemingly infinite particularities of it that can never be exhausted. But if all that "Combray" has to teach us is this kind of aporia, how can the narration come into being? And how does it come out of a "tasse de thé?"

One might argue that the source of the narration is not only "vérité" or any other abstract word in "-té," but also the "thé" itself—the final word of the madeleine episode—as a metaphor for the particular, for everything that perishes in time and that, as Zeno's paradoxes tell us, ultimately proves to be uncapturable by any general principle. But is the entire novel then written under the sign of the particular? Is it simply the story of a series of particular moments uninhabited by any general principle? Before coming to this too-hasty conclusion, let us dwell on the word *tasse*. A cup is a fixed, easily identifiable form that persists in an unchanging state through time. Like what is about to be narrated, it assumes "form and solidity." Moreover—and here I beg the reader's momentary indulgence—the origin of the French suffix "-té" is the Latin "-*tas*" (pronounced like *tasse*). What comes out of Marcel's "tas(se) de t(h)é" is a search for origins and causality, for the very sort of "causal law" that, as we have seen, is the goal of style, metaphor, and involuntary memory.

What the "tas(se) de t(h)é" yields, then, is not a discovery but a search. Proust's narration must be considered as both a search for a general law of causes and origins and a recognition of the finally uncapturable and unrepresentable nature of the temporal—not only of time itself but also of everything that takes place in time. In the opening paragraph of the novel we encounter two words ending in "-té": "the rivalry [*la rivalité*] of François I and Charles V" (1.3) is what the book with which Marcel is reading himself to sleep is said to be about, while the state in which he finds himself upon waking from his half-slumber is "an obscurity [*une obscurité*] gentle and restful for my eyes, but perhaps even more so for my mind, to which it seemed like a thing without a cause [*une chose sans cause*], incomprehensible, a really obscure thing [*une chose vraiment obscure*]" (1.3). One might think that the *obscurité*, insofar as it is an abstract, general term, would be easy to understand, that Marcel's mind might have no difficulty grasping it. But the abstract term here becomes almost immediately concretized: *obscurité* becomes redefined as "une chose vraiment obscure," the abstract term applied to something concrete (cf. "I saw a real beauty walking down the street"), and it is as such, as something concrete and particular, that Marcel cannot understand it. "Une chose sans cause" is doubly a phrase of lost causality, for not only does it explicitly name a loss of causality, but the Latin *causa* is etymologically related to the French *chose*; a "chose sans cause" is a thing that has lost its etymology, its relation to a past. This is a state of nonnarration or prenarration: the book Marcel is reading has already found its abstract law ("rivalité"), but the book he wants to write has not.

In order to discover a law of origins, to answer the question of *why* the madeleine fills him with felicity, the narrator must schematize time; he must take as an axiom the possibility that a given instant goes back to an earlier one that is somehow its source. But if this is the case, then when he begins to try to represent Combray in the framework of a search for origins, he is using the same sort of artifice as Zeno. How, then, does he avoid becoming trapped by Zeno's paradoxes? How can he use the general to reach the particular, or derive the general from the particular?[20]

The answer is that he does not, and cannot. Proust's entire enterprise is Zenonian. It is a chase after a general knowledge of the particular value of what takes place in time, or perhaps a chase after the particular value of what takes place in time using general principles and concepts and even the necessary generality of language itself, for in spite of the vision of a mysterious and utterly particular language glimpsed in "Place-names" ("Noms de pays"), the narrator rejects the idea of writing his novel using only this thoroughly private language. But the chase does not succeed. Nor is it meant to. The genius of Proust's text considered in the light of Zeno's paradoxes is that the text recognizes from the start that it will never catch up with what it is pursuing.

Thus Proust's narrative is profoundly consonant with Zeno's paradoxes, even at the level of what most strikingly characterizes it, its style. Proust's notoriously long and convoluted sentences create the impression of a Zenonian chase. Not only do they often take place within a single moment of time, but they also seem unable to come to a close precisely because they cannot manage to circumscribe what they are quite literally talking "about." The Proustian sentence gives the impression of an infinite narration of a single moment, of an unremitting postponement of the arrival at a goal (the end of the sentence), of a dissatisfaction arising both from the unrepresentability of a single moment and from the unpleasant feeling that no moment ever really "leads" to another moment except by default, or perhaps exhaustion. This is one of a fairly small number of texts—Joyce's *Ulysses* is another prominent example—in which the relation of the time of narration to the time of what is being narrated very often yields a fraction greater than one. And one sometimes gets the feeling that if the narration were allowed free reign, that fraction would tend toward infinity, and the narrative would never move forward at all.

Where Proust goes Zeno one better is that for Proust, Zeno's paradoxes are *not only a painful aporia but also, finally, a source of empowerment*. The text makes fairly clear from the outset that what its protagonist cannot bear, the major source of his anguish and insomnia, is his mortality. Life cannot be infinitely prolonged any more than the power of a used tea bag. But Zeno's paradoxes tell us that even the smallest length of time can be *indefinitely divided from within*; indeed, that because of the limits that hinder the human mind from satisfactorily representing or even understanding temporal movement, time invites the kind of division and subdivision upon which the paradoxes are based.

This, then, is finally the reason why the experience of the madeleine fills Marcel with *félicité* and makes life's *brièveté* illusory: not because it provides Marcel with an unfailing general principle, nor even because it gives him back the past as it was, but rather because it shows him that since one can attempt to represent time only by an infinitely prolongable process of division and analysis, that representation of something finite can itself offer the narrator his own experience of the infinite. The inadequacy of representation through the fixed and general is a source not only of frustration, but also of a kind of immortality from within.

It is in this sense that we may understand the final words of *Le Temps retrouvé* and, consequently, of the entire cycle:

> At least, if [strength] was left me for a long enough time to accomplish my work, in it I would not fail to describe people first of all (even if that were to make them seem like monstrous beings) as occupying a very considerable place, compared to the restrained one that is reserved for them in space, a place on the contrary prolonged without measure—since they touch simultaneously, like giants plunged into the years, such distant eras, between which so many days have come to place themselves—in Time. (3.1048)

The narrator's goal identifies the novel as a Zenonian undertaking, but one that takes Zeno's paradoxes as allies, almost as founding principles. If the characters in Proust's novel are "prolonged without measure," it is not, as the scenes of teetering old people in *Le Temps retrouvé* make clear, because they are immortal. Rather the narrator, himself a mortal whose "stilts" are "already so high" (3.1048) that he perhaps rightly fears that not much more time will be needed to topple him, is the one who prolongs his representation of them without measure. Even the style of this final passage, which is quite characteristic of the style of the novel as a whole, is decidedly Zenonian. This last, long sentence seems not to want to come to an end, and it is constructed as a series of intruding insertions—a parenthetical phrase, one set off by dashes, others set off by commas—that, like the moments of time being spoken of in the sentence itself, "place themselves" between the endpoints of the sentence and prevent it from coming to an end.

But this postponement is a blessing, since this is, of course, the single sentence of Proust that we least want to end, it being the last one of the entire work. For anyone who, like Swann falling in love with Odette, has been changed reading the novel without quite being able to say when or how, reaching the end in this way offers a final comforting lesson, one worthy of Proust's peculiarly benign Zeno: if we cannot adequately represent change, at least we can "lose" our mortality— both "waste" the time allotted to us (what Proust might call, in a positive sense, *perdre notre temps*) and find a paradoxical kind of immortality—in the attempt.

Chapter 4

FICTION AND FILM:

PROUST'S VERTIGO AND HITCHCOCK'S *VERTIGO*

A Vertiginous *Recherche*

THE IDEA OF MAKING a film version of Proust's cycle of novels has tempted a number of prominent figures, from Pinter (who wrote a screenplay for a film of Proust that has never been produced) to Pasolini (who died before he could realize his project). But the novel presents formidable problems to anyone undertaking such a task, and particularly from the point of view of the novel's peculiar temporality: relatively little actually happens in this mammoth work—and, what is worse from a cinematic point of view, it takes a very long time not to happen.

Volker Schlöndorff's recent film of *Un Amour de Swann* (1983) only underscores the difficulties of filming Proust. A meticulous costume drama of almost unremitting angst,[1] the film is especially unsuccessful in its treatment of temporality. Not only does it persist in eliminating Proust's temporal tricks and replacing them with a coherent, straightforward narrative, but it also essentially fetishizes the time period in which the story is set; whatever little impact the film does have is based on the titillating questions of what Proust's characters might actually have looked like,[2] how they would have dressed, in what sort of carriages they might have traveled around Paris, and in what style they would have been likely to decorate their homes.[3] While it might well be argued that Proust himself fetishizes the 1870s and 1880s in his novel[4]—indeed, that period is undoubtedly one of the things referred to by the "Lost Time" of the cycle's title—his work is designed less to arouse a lurid curiosity about those decades within its readers than to set them to thinking about the nature of temporality itself.

I propose, in this chapter, that a far more interesting interaction between Proust's novel and cinema—one that is centered around the very question of temporality that Schlöndorff evades—can be found in the 1958 Alfred Hitchcock film, *Vertigo*. It is true that finding any relation between Proust's *Recherche* and Hitchcock's film may itself seem a vertiginous search. *Vertigo*, often called Hitchcock's masterpiece,[5] has been compared to such literary models as the tales of Orpheus and Eurydice,

Pygmalion and Galatea, Tristan and Isolde,[6] Adam and Lilith, and Faust, but no one to my knowledge has made explicit reference to Proust as a possible source. Thomas Narcejac, the co-author of the French novel, *D'Entre les morts*[7] (since rebaptized *Sueurs froides* after the French title of the Hitchcock film), upon which the film is based, assures me that in writing his novel he had Orpheus in mind and not Marcel.[8] Indeed, in many ways Proust's work and Hitchcock's are diametrically opposed. Where might we find a common thread between Proust's novel, which is so adamantly subjective that it resists all attempts to narrate its "events," which is built upon a series of flights of fancy and endlessly prolonged metaphors, which takes no time to sum up and a lifetime to read, and Hitchcock's cinema, often taken as a model of narrative technique, an art that, in the space of two hours, always tells a story, and generally does so with such economy and concentration that it sometimes gives the impression of being filmed by an objective, impersonal force?[9]

But this incongruity between Proust and Hitchcock provides much of the interest of discussing them together, for it is closely related to the larger question of Proust's compatibility (or incompatibility) with cinema. After all, Hitchcock has been recognized as not only one of the greatest of the century's filmmakers, but also one of the most profoundly cinematic. How, then, can we find the spirit of Proust within a work of Hitchcock's in spite of the difficulty of translating Proust into the medium of film?

HITCHCOCK'S MADELEINE: *VERTIGO* AND TIME

A number of elements in *Vertigo* make it difficult to ignore Proust as a subtext of the film. Samuel Taylor, the main author of the screenplay, informs me that he read Proust some ten years before working on the film.[10] But first and foremost, the film's heroine is named "Madeleine Elster," combining the name of Proust's famous memory-jolting cake with that of the narrator's favorite painter in Proust's novel,[11] and this name is only half-provided by *D'Entre les morts*, in which the heroine is named (or rather poses as someone who is named) Madeleine Gévigne. And as we briefly recount the film's plot, the impact of this combination becomes apparent.

Scottie, a San Francisco cop, has acute acrophobia after unwittingly causing a fatal fall. Having retired from the police force, he is approached by Gavin Elster, an old friend who claims that his wife, Madeleine, is acting strangely and needs to be followed. Scottie reluctantly agrees to follow her and then, in the process, falls in love with her. Madeleine Elster, it seems, is possessed by the spirit of her great-grandmother, Carlotta Valdes, who went insane and committed suicide; Madeleine, in a trance, regularly visits a museum to sit in front of Carlotta's portrait, and models her hairstyle, culminating in a vertiginous bun, after this painting. She dreams of a Spanish-style mission with a bell tower, and Scottie, recognizing her description as that of a mission one hundred miles south of the city, takes her there, hoping to free her of her tortured past. But he is unable to stop her from jumping from the tower to her death, because his vertigo prevents him from following her to the top of the stairs.

In the second half of the film, after more or less recovering from a mental collapse, Scottie meets Judy Barton, a woman who closely resembles Madeleine (both characters are played by Kim Novak). Although Judy proves to him that she is not Madeleine Elster, Scottie becomes obsessed with her because of her resemblance to Madeleine and begins to spend all of his time with her. Meanwhile we are told, by means of a letter that we see Judy write to Scottie but not send, that Judy is Madeleine, that she was hired by Gavin Elster to play the role of his wife in an elaborate murder scheme. The woman who fell to her death was the real Madeleine Elster;[12] Judy Barton, posing as her, simply ran to the top of the bell tower from which Gavin Elster then threw his wife's dead body. Judy is nonetheless really in love with Scottie, and in spite of her fear of discovery, she decides to try to make him love her as she is. But soon he makes known his wish to transform her into the woman he has lost, and, with her reluctant consent, he makes her over into Madeleine, with identical clothing and hairstyle. Immediately following his reunion with his remade "Madeleine," he notices that she is wearing a necklace resembling the one in the Carlotta Valdes portrait, and this slipup makes him realize that this *is* the first Madeleine. He takes Judy back to the mission at night to force a confession out of her, drags her up to the tower, and, after her confession, watches in horror as, startled by the voice of a nun, she falls to her death from the tower.

Hitchcock's "Madeleine," like Proust's, is thus the embodiment of the central experience of reliving the past. Perhaps the major character of the film, as of the novel, is time: the entire second half of the film describes Scottie's attempt to re-create the past. He, too, is going after lost time, albeit, as we shall see, in a way that distinguishes him from Proust's hero. The power of vertigo comes from the incongruity of feeling one's finite being, limited in time and space, in the dizzying presence of the infinite, the abyss. We can hardly imagine a more heartbreakingly powerful image of lost time and its irretrievability than that of the film's falling scenes, in which Scottie, unlike the filmmaker, cannot reverse the sequence and watch the dead spring back to life. That after Madeleine's fall Scottie is living in a postlapsarian world is suggested by the location of Judy Barton's hotel, on "Post" Street:[13] after the fall there is only a feeling of nostalgia, a feeling that it is too late.

Thus, once Scottie has lost Madeleine, his desire can move only backward, but time continues to move forward. At the film's narrative midpoint, when Scottie makes a heart-rending pilgrimage back to Madeleine's apartment building, the image of a one-way sign fills much of the screen for no less than twenty seconds, and its lesson is the lesson of mortality: that time is irreversible. Scottie has a one-way or one-track mind in the second half of the film. He is possessed—indeed, ultimately obsessed—by the past.

In spite of the similarity of Madeleine's and the madeleine's relation to time in the film and in the novel, respectively, their actual functions are opposite in the two works. If Marcel, Proust's protagonist, relives the past when he partakes of the madeleine, if this teaches him that the past contains hidden, unexpected secrets, then he ultimately realizes at the end of the novel that being obsessed with the past and with extracting its riches will be the highest expression of his mortal state, of the endless series of habits that characterize his own mortality as much as they do Aunt Léonie's. In Scottie's case the reverse is true: he knows from the start that his vertigo is a result of a past trauma that he cannot escape, and if he falls in love with Madeleine it is largely because she, too, appears to be haunted and trapped by the past. The narration of the sequence of events leading to Madeleine's death opens at the moment when Scottie, physically recovered from his trauma, is about to throw away his cane and his corset, and can thus say, "Tomorrow I will be a free man"; but this physical liberation does not mean he is in fact any less constrained by the past. In this same early scene, in which Scottie's college sweetheart, Midge, plays the role of a protective mother, Scottie tries briefly to end his enslavement to the past—that is, his vertigo—by getting used to heights little by little, by the mechanism, so important in Proust, of habit. The masculine world of the ladder in the opening scene of the trauma is replaced by a kitchen stool,[14] and Scottie tries to go up step by step, only to fall faintly into Midge's arms, his experiment with habit a failure. Where habit generally hides the passage of time in Proust—indeed, the narrator first finds "lost time" by consuming his madeleine and his tea "against his habit"[15]—its failure here indicates the undomesticable nature of time and of the past for Scottie.

One of the film's central images is that of viewing things from behind, figuratively, the perspective of the past; in a brief comic interlude, Midge, a fashion designer, banters about a new brassière she is sketching that is based on the model of the cantilever bridge[16] and features something called "revolutionary uplift," that is, no visible support from the back. But this moment of levity actually holds one of the film's keys: Scottie falls in love with Madeleine from the back,[17] while he is following her. In the first scene in which he sees her, he gazes at her back—indeed, in her strapless, low-cut dress she seems to be wearing the "revolutionary uplift" brassière herself—and he even avoids looking her directly in the face when she approaches.[18] Madeleine thus instantly represents Scottie's own limitations and his desire to transcend them; because he sees her from the back, she seems to look only ahead and to have no need of support from the back or the past, and thus represents Scottie's own potential liberation from the world of temporality.

Scottie wants to liberate Madeleine from the past. He takes her to the old Spanish mission in the hope that remembering the place will free her from the tortured image of it about which she dreams, and he undoubtedly thinks that if he can free Madeleine of the past, perhaps he can free himself from it as well. Scottie's losing Madeleine and his subsequent descent into madness tell him that his first attempt to cure the past is not feasible; another solution must be found.

The Limits of Fiction in Film

That other solution is art: if Scottie is a victim of the past in the first half of the film, he espouses the past in the second half by re-creating it. By making life into art, and Judy into Madeleine, he wants to control and freeze the passage of time. In Proust's terms Scottie's error would be that he uses *voluntary* memory to impart to the second Madeleine the force of the first; indeed, he offers Madeleine coffee, the beverage of the will, no less than four times but does not think to offer her a tisane. It may seem surprising, then, that Scottie is in fact satisfied with his re-creation of Madeleine. But what Scottie wants is not what Marcel wants: Scottie wants *not* to recapture time in its essence, but rather to stop it. He wants Madeleine to become a static image, and the film to turn into a photograph, or, better yet, a painting.

And it is here that the second half of Madeleine Elster's name, the name of Proust's painter, takes on its full importance. Not only is Madeleine modeled after a painting, but Scottie attempts to re-create her as a sort of living painting based on his memory of her, the element of will involved in the transformation being the only thing that allows him to go on in a world without her. Scottie's excessive ambition, to make art correspond exactly to life and control it, is in fact also the path to both his and Madeleine's downfall. What gives Judy away is that she too-closely resembles art, since at the climactic moment, when the artistic transformation to Madeleine is complete, she puts on the necklace from the Carlotta painting that proves her criminal link to the real Madeleine Elster, to the Madeleine who cannot be brought back from the dead, art notwithstanding. What Judy forgets is that Madeleine is not simply, as in Proust, a means to reach the domain of art; she is also, in Hitchcock, the articulation between art and criminality, the character whose art is a result and a function of her involvement in a crime and whose crime is that she allows life to resemble art just a little too much, to be revealed as artifice. What Scottie, like Judy but unlike Marcel, wants is *not* to open up Madeleine and see the essence that she contains—for her hidden message is the emptiness of mortality, the inescapable abyss, the cause of vertigo—but rather to capture only her external form, to dress her up as what she is not.

It is in this sense that another central opposition in Proust also works in the film: painting and music, which both characterize Swann's love for Odette but in different ways. Swann's love comes to be expressed by Vinteuil's little phrase, the repetition through time of the melody of their meetings—and music is thus essentially an expression of rhythm and temporality. Odette also reminds Swann of a painting, but it is precisely the difference between her and it that makes him desire her: it is the element of artifice, the need to re-create her in the image of a Botticelli, that attracts him to someone who is "not his type."

In the film, Scottie's "type" is nothing but artifice itself, embodied by painting. Midge, whose abandonment of painting as a career suggests her directness, her refusal of artifice that is precisely what makes her unappealing to Scottie,[19] loses him even as a friend by painting a satirical portrait of Carlotta with her own practical, bespectacled face in the place of Carlotta's ethereal one. By contrast, music and sound are what threaten Scottie's artificial world; as Donald Spoto puts it, "Throughout the film voices attempt to break through Scottie's sealed fantasy world,"[20] what readers of Proust might consider his cork-lined room. Thus Scottie says only half-jokingly that Midge's Mozart recording is making him dizzy, music once again being associated with the vertigo of temporality,[21] as opposed to the unchanging nature of the imperishable, timeless image. Later, when Midge visits Scottie in the mental hospital after his breakdown, she tries to "cure" him with recordings of Mozart, as if to bring him back to the world of the temporal, and in her final words on-screen she admits dejectedly that Mozart will never do a thing to help him to forget Madeleine. One of the first times Scottie and Madeleine look at each other face-to-face they are interrupted by the noise of the telephone, and after Madeleine's "suicide," Judy's most obvious flaw is her exaggeratedly coarse voice: in spite of her visual resemblance to Madeleine, it is her voice that makes her mortal. Even Madeleine's final fall into mortality, Judy's death-plunge from the church tower, is precipitated by a nun's intruding voice.

Does this mean that Scottie might have been better off in a silent film, just as Swann might have done better as a music critic than as an art critic? If cinema is the marriage of image and sound, perhaps one final image, an image that also makes a sound, the church's bell tower, might help us to close our discussion of *Vertigo*. A church tower one hundred miles south of the city: does the mission at San Juan Bautista not recall Proust's famous *clocher de Saint-Hilaire*? In the film, the final violent scene in the bell tower is what finally cures Scottie's vertigo,[22] as he manages to reach the top of the staircase and, once Judy has confessed and fallen to her death, looks down from the tower in the film's final frame. What cures Scottie's vertigo is his understanding of the relation of the two halves of the film, of art to life. If vertigo was for Scottie the feeling of the incongruity of the relation between the limits of mortal existence and any experience of the infinite, the sensation that the timeless and the mortal, or perhaps God and humanity, belong to two radically incompatible worlds, then his vertigo ends when he gives up any ambition of ever joining them. At the beginning of the film, Scottie jokingly mentions crossing the Golden Gate Bridge as the ultimate test of being cured of vertigo, and what does in fact cure it is letting go of any future attempt to bridge the finite and the infinite, giving up the "revolutionary uplift" based on the design of a bridge. "Madeleine" is punished for her fiction, and Scottie for believing in it and trying to carry it even further, and that fiction has to do with appropriating the divine power of taking life or re-creating it. *Vertigo* is a film in which it is a crime to bring life back through fiction.

In Proust the bell tower is also associated with death: Aunt Léonie is petrified at the idea of climbing it partly because from its heights "certain people claim to have felt the coldness of death" (1.106), but also because reaching its peak is analogous to being able to observe the terrifying passage of time in the town below, and even in one's own day-to-day life. It is for this reason that at the end of Proust's novel, Marcel's final epiphany, his decision to write his novel, is a form of vertigo: tripping on two uneven paving stones reminds him, in an experience similar to tasting the madeleine, of the baptistry of Saint Mark in Venice. The church tower in *Vertigo* also carries the idea of baptism—"San Juan Bautista"—but whereas the divine presence or perhaps the divine ambition in the film is what is ultimately inaccessible through fiction, Marcel's epiphany puts him close to the gods, and does not cure him of vertigo, but rather imposes it on him:

I had an impression of weariness and fear as I felt that . . . at every instant I had to keep all of this length of time attached to myself, that it was holding me up, perched at its vertiginous peak [*son sommet vertigineux*]. . . . I had vertigo [*J'avais le vertige*] as I saw below me, and yet within me, as if I were miles high, so many years. (3.1047)

Marcel's "revolutionary uplift" is the belief—whether or not it is shared by the reader—that he *can* be supported from behind, that the past can be a source of transcendence. Until he (re)tastes the madeleine, Marcel's relation to his past is based upon a static verticality, as his memories of his childhood are limited to the line of descent from his bedroom upstairs to the dining room downstairs from which his mother may or may not come up to give him his good-night kiss.[23] All of his horizontal displacements in the social world, the widening of his horizons, can tell him nothing about this vertical structure. Only eating the madeleine allows him to give himself up to an utterly unstable verticality, to vertigo itself, and to exploring the nature of the passage of time, the relation between the generations, whether that relation is situated between the adults' ground-floor dining room and his own childhood fantasies of joining their world, or between his nighttime solitary vigils as an old man and the memories of youth that inhabit them. If vertigo is, for Marcel as for Scottie, the feeling of incongruity between mortality and anything that goes beyond mortality—be it the desire to resurrect the dead or that of bringing the past to life—what Marcel finally accepts as the highest possible expression of mortal existence is fiction, the inadequacy of which is precisely what in the film takes Madeleine away.

The Limits of Film in Fiction

Thus Marcel begins to write his novel where Hitchcock ends his film, and we might extend this chiasmus by adding that if Proust's novel anticipates the cinematic future and presents it with one of its most enduring challenges, the only flashback in Hitchcock's film shows the death of the real Madeleine. It is as if the novel and the film were reaching toward each other, each wanting what the other has: the Hitchcock film needs an unshakable belief in fiction, a re-creatable Madeleine, and what Proust longs for in his novel is to animate his series of images and give them the kinetic and cinematic dimensions lacking in fiction.

This is not to say that Proust simply valorizes cinema over fiction. If in Proust's novel ongoing perception is opposed to retrospective comprehension-through-literature as the photographic negative [*cliché*][24] is opposed to "developed" negatives (presumably photographs),[25] the final step in this "development" through time might be expected to be cinema. But Proust criticizes "a simple cinematographic vision" (3.889) precisely because cinema cannot render what he calls life's "thickness," the always complex and often contradictory components of a given moment. When he says that the novel should not be "a sort of cinematographic procession [*défilé*] of things" because "nothing could be further from what we have perceived in reality than such a cinematographic view" (3.882–83), he is perhaps neglecting the fact that "what we have perceived in reality" is in some respects not the model for the novel, and that our perceptions in time are indeed very much like cinema. In the final step of the progression from negative to photograph to cinema, there is an extra dimension of *uniform* temporality—one can peruse photos at one's leisure, but a film passes by at a steady, unremitting pace—and Proust's novel repeatedly shows us the falsity of "a uniform painting [*peinture uniforme*] of life" (3.870).

Cinema, far from being the ultimate model of comprehension, may in fact be taken as a metaphor for life *as it is lived* in Proust. Life in Proust is cinematic insofar as it is, as we saw in Chapter 3, discontinuous—since time moves "forward" only thanks to the miniscule jumps between frames—and at the same time based on an illusion of continuity—on changes from moment to moment or from frame to frame that are so gradual as to be imperceptible. Because it moves across these tiny "breaks," life as Proust depicts it is both fundamentally disunified and resistant to the *profound* discontinuity of metaphor, the extracting of meaning through distance and difference (3.889), which requires the kind of doubling-back that is the precondition of involuntary memory. Life-as-cinema refuses to stop and allow us to surround an individual moment with depth, with multiple perspectives. If, as Georges Poulet puts it, the real significance of Proustian space is made up of "the totality of . . . perspectives, as in those cubist paintings in which the painter tries to give at one and the same time all those aspects of an object which one could ordinarily discover in it only by viewing it turn by turn at different angles,"[26] cinema is precisely the medium that resists this totality, for while one may have many photographs of a single model taken simultaneously, each frame in a cinematic sequence is temporally unique.[27]

As was discussed in Chapter 3, when Swann is about to kiss Odette for the first time and thus move into a new stage of his life, he feels the need to do what a film director might call "stopping the action"; he holds Odette's face between his hands: "Swann was the one who, before [Odette] let [her face] fall, as if in spite of herself, onto his lips, held it an instant, at some distance from himself, in his two hands" (1.233). It is as if Swann were trying to turn the ongoing cinema of life into a series of snapshots that, from Zeno's point of view, would be much more easily comprehensible than a film. Analogously, when Marcel kisses Albertine for the first time, the kiss is described as if, in the flickering light of an early film, Marcel were seeing the separate frames that made up the movement of his face toward Albertine's: "in this short trip of my lips toward her cheek, it is ten Albertines that I saw" (2.365). In the intervening years between Swann's and Odette's first kiss and that of Marcel and Albertine, cinema has actually come into being, and the jerky, uneven movements of early films are a wonderful metaphor for Marcel's dissatisfaction not only with this first kiss, but also with life's general insistence on moving forward before one is quite ready to follow it. This constant movement of cinema is the very model of life as it is lived: unseizable and incomprehensible, Albertine is "unfixable" by anything but fiction.

Thus Proust's fiction takes as one of its central premises the freedom of a noncinematic, nonuniform temporal displacement (that is, twenty pages on a single moment); but can life's cinematic aspect ever be completely "corrected" by the fiction of the novel? The end of Proust's novel allows—even requires—the reader to return to the beginning, to reverse narrative time and start all over, and this reversal is the premise, indeed the epitome of his fiction: rereading Proust's novel with the knowledge of its end only enriches the fictional reading of a life that, without its (re)constitution as a fiction, would be infinitely poorer. To this extent, such fiction might even be called "anticinematic." And yet does the fiction of the novel ever fully stop yearning for the very cinema, the irrepressible and irreversible movement that it is trying to "fix"?

This inextricable yearning for movement is most apparent in the character of Albertine. From her first appearance in the novel, pushing a bicycle (1.788), Albertine is the embodiment of speed and motion. Even before she appears she is described as being "très 'fast'" (1.512). When Marcel keeps her waiting one day, Françoise laconically sums up the girl's character in this way: "With a speedy one like her, she's probably gone already. She doesn't like to wait" (2.777). In spite of her numerous appearances in the novel, Albertine leaves the impression of having sped through all her scenes, and the fact that Marcel finally feels the need to imprison her in his apartment further suggests that what he must take control of is what most centrally characterizes Albertine, her movements. Her death a very short time after she escapes her imprisonment is caused by this very speediness: she is thrown from a horse and hits a tree (3.476); even in death she represents the conflict between the moving and the fixed. As we saw in Chapter 2, the loss of Albertine is essential if Marcel is to become a narrator and is thus a necessary precondition of Proust's fiction. But is this not a fiction that knows—even if it may refuse to acknowledge it openly—that something has been lost, that in "fixing" (both stabilizing and repairing) time, it has had to give up the ambitions proper to a different mode of representation, that of cinema, which tries to represent movement itself?

In an essay published only a few years after Proust's death, Ramon Fernandez succinctly characterizes Proust's entire novelistic enterprise in terms that suggest the limitations of his fiction:

> For Proust ... [to keep an impression] is to fuse one's ego entirely in the experience, to deposit this ego at the points of time and space where the experience has taken place, and thereby *to cut it up into pieces each of which is identified with a particular experience and lodged in a corner of time which thus acquires a fixity and an externality which are characters proper to space*. ... [Proust affirms] that the different parts of time are reciprocally exclusive and remain external to one another.[28]

As the narrator looks back on his life, he finds that it is divided up into discrete moments, or "corners of time." Not only does he have only intermittent access to those moments through involuntary memory, but the moments themselves do not seem to communicate with one another, so that he is reduced to wondering whether it is possible to move from one point in time to another.

Even though the narrator strongly criticizes the kind of literature that "is satisfied with 'describing things,'" on the grounds that such literature "abruptly cuts off all communication of our present self with the past ... and the future" (3.885), and even though Proust's novel is in some respects about the passage of time, it nonetheless depicts a series of static and discrete moments that provide no apparent means of linkage among them. As Georges Poulet puts it:

> [In Proust's novel] what we find only very infrequently is the continuous progression of beings in their physical and spiritual lives, the reasons that push them to abandon their earlier positions [*cadres*] and to take up new ones. In short, the only images of themselves that Proust's characters are allowed to offer us are like those snapshots of a single person that fill our photo albums. Here he is at one time of his life, then at another; there she is in the city, in the country, in evening clothes, in a housedress. Each of these "snapshots" is rigorously determined by its framing [*cadre*]; the whole remains discontinuous.[29]

The *cadres* or frameworks about which Poulet speaks here are attempts to quantify change by means of a series of states. But, as we saw in Chapter 3, a series of states tells us nothing at all about movement. Proust's narrator may well be empowered by the essentially Zenonian conclusion that "even if they led me toward nothing, these instants [that I remembered] seemed to me to be sufficiently charming in themselves" (1.426); nonetheless, such "leading toward nothing" still constitutes one of the limits of his fiction: the impossibility of representing movement.

To return, in conclusion, to Hitchcock: when his film ends at the very moment of recognizing its inability to hold onto a fiction, is it, too, not naming *its* loss? Although its beauties become only more evident as the film is seen again and again, *Vertigo* nonetheless loses a central element after the first viewing. Once Scottie's eyes (and ours) have been opened, once he sees what it is that he has loved and lost, and we see that he has seen it, *Vertigo* can never be the same experience again. Proust's novel can *only* be reread, but Hitchcock's film, which is built around the impossibility of return, even in an artistic mode, can never really be seen a second time.

Perhaps, then, Hitchcock's Madeleine and her untimely death can help us realize why an eminently cinematic figure like Hitchcock, and perhaps even the narrative cinema of which he is increasingly recognized as the master, are not only incompatible with Proust's fiction, but might also for this very reason be said to have given us, with *Vertigo*, a sort of cinematic version of that fiction, or rather of what limits it, of what it can never have—movement itself—any more than Scottie can keep Madeleine as a (reversible) fiction. If translating Proust's novel of temporality into film seems to have offered cinema one of its most tempting goals, perhaps the irony is that, like many of Marcel's dreams and ambitions, and even his dream of writing a novel, it has already been realized. Or, more precisely, the reasons why it can never be satisfactorily realized have themselves furnished the matter of a film, long ago.

PART III
LOVE AND DEATH

Chapter 5

PROUST AND WAGNER:

THE CLIMB TO THE OCTAVE ABOVE,
OR, THE SCALE OF LOVE (AND DEATH)

THE CLIMB TO THE OCTAVE ABOVE

PROUST'S INTEREST in music has been well documented. Georges Piroué, for example, organizes an entire section of his study around what he considers to be the "musical structure" of Proust's novel.[1] In this chapter I will explore the interaction between Proust's twentieth-century masterpiece of French fiction and a work by a German composer who is among the greatest European musicians of the nineteenth century, Richard Wagner. The links between Proust and Wagner are numerous and complex; indeed, many pages have been devoted to this relation, including Emile Bedriomo's recent study, *Proust, Wagner, et la coïncidence des arts*.[2] This chapter is not intended to synthesize the considerable work that has already been done on the relations between Proust's fictional universe and Wagner's musical one, but rather to focus attention on a very particular point of intersection between Proust's novel and a passage from Wagner's *Tristan and Isolde*. More specifically, I will examine the ways in which Proust's text uses certain associations with *Tristan and Isolde* in its own working-out of the relation between love and death.

In order to structure my discussion around the text's own terms, I will concentrate on a particular musical interval—the octave, which plays an important function in the musical diatonic scale—and on the ways it comes to organize certain key questions in Proust's novel. As will probably be clear from the nature of the specific passages and examples analyzed, this organization around the octave, as well as the text's associations with *Tristan*, is probably at least partly subconscious on Proust's part. And in the work of a novelist who spends a good deal of his time analyzing many of the major developments of his own novel with a remarkable—but, from an aesthetic point of view, at times excessive—self-awareness, it is all the more powerful for being so.

The octave is first mentioned when the narrator's grandmother observes the church tower of Saint-Hilaire:

And as she looked at it, as her eyes followed the gentle tension, the fervent inclination of its stony slopes narrowing as they went up like hands clasped in prayer, she joined so fully with the effusiveness [*effusion*] of the spire that her gaze seemed to soar up with it; and at the same time she smiled warmly at the old worn-out stones the top of which was the only thing lit up by the sunset and that, when they entered this sunny zone, softened by light, seemed suddenly mounted [*montées*] much higher up, distant, like a song repeated in "head voice," an octave above [*une octave au-dessus*].[3]

The top of the tower is said to be like a voice singing an "octave above" the rest of the building, and this simile has considerable ramifications for Proust's entire novel. For the grandmother, who is mysteriously united with the spire as she looks at it, the image of the climb ("montées") to the octave above already gives us its two principal values. First, the octave above is a difficult and distant goal, and the grandmother, by aiming to reach it, seems to be trying to rise above Combray's humdrum world of routine and repetition. Second, if indeed she completes the climb to the octave above, she can allow herself an unaccustomed expression of emotion, an "effusiveness." For if, as the grandmother speculates in another musical metaphor, the church tower would not play the piano "drily" ("s'il jouait du piano, il ne jouerait pas *sec*," 1.64), she herself appears to join it here in an unusual outpouring of feeling. These two values of the octave, the difficult and painful climb up the scale toward the octave above and the inhabitual expression of emotion if one ever reaches it, will organize our discussion; both of them have far-reaching implications for Proust's undertaking.

"TRISTE" AND "ISOLÉ"

Let us begin by examining the two characters who are vehemently opposed to the grandmother's desire to climb to the octave above: Tante Léonie and Marcel. Tante Léonie, far from admiring the top of the church tower, is horrified at the curé's mere suggestion that she might ever have the strength of will to climb the ninety-seven steps leading up to it and enjoy the view that rewards such a climb (1.105–6). If the top of the church tower is an octave above the everyday life of Combray, then Tante Léonie prefers the drone of her own stultifying existence. It is thus particularly important to recall that Tante Léonie's late husband is in fact *named* Octave; indeed, the old lady is often addressed as "Madame Octave."[4] Octave appears to his wife and wants to force her to take a daily walk to stir her from her lethargy (1.109–10); the very thought of this submission to Octave's wishes chills Tante Léonie to the marrow of her bed-ridden bones, as she undoubtedly believes that letting herself be chided into even such a modest level of exertion might one day lead to the walk up the stairs to the top of the church tower that the curé has so tactlessly mentioned. For Léonie, then, the octave—as a concept and also as a character—stands for anything or anyone that might pull her out of herself and her obsessive little routine. Let us recall that "scale" and the French word for staircase, *escalier*, are etymologically related; the steps leading up to the church tower are, metaphorically, a scale leading up to the dreaded octave at the top.

Yet another, even more important character who at least initially resists the climb up toward the octave above is Marcel, the protagonist of Proust's novel. One of the first times that we see Marcel as a young boy, he is unhappily walking up a stairway, having been sent to bed early because of Swann's visit to the house in Combray:

> I had to go up every step of the staircase, as the saying goes, "against my heart," climbing against my heart, which wanted to go back to my mother because she had not, by kissing me, given it permission to follow me. That hateful staircase I always took so sadly [*si tristement*] gave off a smell of varnish that had somehow absorbed and fixed the special kind of suffering that I felt each evening. (1.27–28)

Marcel here is following the model of Tante Léonie, rather than that of his grandmother; the stairway becomes an object of fear and loathing, as it represents the path that he must take to leave behind his own obsession, his mother. Marcel would do anything to avoid taking this staircase, just as Tante Léonie would to get out of climbing up toward the octave; because he is forced by others (rather than by an act of his own will) to climb it evening after evening, it never helps him to resist his obsessive attachment to his mother. On the contrary, the staircase itself becomes an obsessive memory. When the narrator thinks back on Combray, all he can remember is this thin staircase, "always seen at the same hour, isolated [*isolé*] from anything that might be around it, highlighted against the darkness, the bare minimum of scenery . . . for the drama of my undressing; as if Combray had consisted of nothing but two stories linked by a thin staircase" (1.43–44). The terms "triste" (or rather "tristement") and "isolé," whose importance will become clear a little later in our development, are both linked to the hated staircase.

Madame Amédée

Let us now return to the character who best exemplifies the climb toward the octave above, the character who probably would not be afraid to walk up the ninety-seven steps to the top of the church tower: the narrator's grandmother. The grandmother is perhaps the only major character in the novel who seems successful in resisting her own potential obsession, that is, her overpowering attachment to her family; although she is as tender-hearted as Marcel, she refuses to coddle her grandson, and imposes upon herself an almost classical reserve. From the first time we see her, the grandmother is associated with resisting any act of self-indulgence; in fact, the role that Tante Léonie's husband Octave plays for her is one that the grandmother plays for her own husband, Amédée—who, in the few scenes in which he appears, seems to be a model of self-indulgence. In one of the novel's first scenes, his wife vainly tries to prevent him from indulging in cognac (1.11–12), and in general Marcel considers him to be as indulgent of others as he is of himself.[5] When the grandfather confronts his wife's two sisters about their absurdly understated thanking of Swann for his wine (1.34), two world-views collide: the grandmother's sisters, who are like caricatures of their more complex but essentially similar sister, make an almost pathological use of understatement because of their exaggerated fear of any direct expression of sentiment, whereas the grandfather is characterized by an easygoing *laissez-aller*.

This confrontation of personality types is clearest at the moment of the grandmother's death—to which we will return—when the two sisters refuse to come to their sister's bedside, purportedly because they have found "an artist" to play them Beethoven's chamber music in Combray (2.325, 343–44) but actually, we suspect, because they are as terrified at the thought of expressing their feelings for their dying sister as they are of openly showing their gratitude and affection for Swann. The grandfather, at the same time that he indulgently refuses to judge his sisters-in-law, melodramatically expresses his shock at their reticence: "'My poor wife, she was so fond of them,' said my grandfather, wiping away a tear. 'I suppose we shouldn't hold it against them, I've always said they're stark raving mad'" (2.343–44). For Marcel's great-aunts, music is thus an alternative to the expression of emotion, a refuge against its potential power, in the same way that the grandmother's climb toward the octave above is a metaphor for the resistance of the power of her emotional attachment to her family.

Of course music is by no means systematically associated with self-restraint and inhibition in Proust's novel; on the contrary, it is sometimes related to the expression of emotion, as we shall see. What will in fact provide us with an articulation between the climb toward the upper octave—the resistance of potentially overpowering emotions—and the reaching of it—the inhabitual release and expression of emotion—is another term with musical associations, the name "Amédée," which is, for the grandmother, a term corresponding to Léonie's "Octave." The name suggests a link between the grandmother, "Madame Amédée," and Wolfgang Amadeus Mozart, which is certainly fitting in terms of the grandmother's classical tastes and her general reserve and restraint. Moreover, in an earlier version of the scene of the good-night kiss in *Jean Santeuil*, Proust specifically draws a contrast between his hero and the young Mozart[6] who, as is well known, was unremittingly driven by his father as a child to develop his artistic potential—precisely what does *not* happen to the young protagonist of Proust's novel. Indeed, Marcel's constant and indefinite postponement of his artistic vocation is one of his grandmother's greatest disappointments (1.580); more specifically "Madame Amédée" seems to live up to her name in her desire to impose, if not quite a Mozart-like regimen on her grandson, at least a strict and disciplined one that might give him some much-needed strength, as her first words in the novel already indicate: "'That's not the way to make him hale and hearty,' she would say sadly, 'especially this little one who so needs to build up his strength and will'" (1.11). To this extent the name "Amédée" seems to be associated with the climb toward the upper octave—that is, with the unremitting effort to subordinate one's feelings to a higher goal.

In an essay written in 1895, Proust, describing Camille Saint-Saëns playing a Mozart piano concerto, defends the pianist-composer against the public's reaction that he played Mozart "too drily" ("il a joué trop sec"[7]), thereby anticipating what will later be Madame Amédée's impression that the church tower, were it to play the piano, would *not* play drily ("il ne jouerait pas *sec*," 1.64), and it is here that we begin to see the double value of Madame Amédée's climb toward the octave above. While the grandmother's own strategy of self-resistance at times makes her seem "dry," what she values in the top of the church tower is not only its singing an octave higher, but also its *not* playing drily. Self-restraint (the climb to the octave above) seems to have value only insofar as it leads to an eventual release of emotion (not playing drily, related to the "effusiveness" of the church tower, 1.64). How and why is this so?

Let us first recall that the model for *Monsieur* Amédée, Monsieur Sandré, the grandfather in *Jean Santeuil*, is even stricter than Madame Amédée in the *Recherche*, but when Jean tells him in a fit of rage that he hates him, the grandfather, *while listening to Mozart*, melts in an inhabitual expression of emotion, sitting Jean down on his lap and kissing him "with his old hardened lips."[8] This scene has an important relation to the character of Madame Amédée: although Marcel's grandmother in the *Recherche* is, unlike Monsieur Sandré, gentle even in her sternness and reserve, both sides of Monsieur Sandré—his usual reserve and his unusual effusiveness—are in fact essential components of her character. It is because the grandmother habitually refuses to indulge her soft-heartedness—the climb to the upper octave as self-resistance—that when she finally does let out all her pent-up emotion, she reaches something akin to a musical resolution to the tonic, a powerful release of anticipation and tension: when one reaches the octave after climbing a musical scale, one feels one has earned a long-awaited rest.

If the grandmother's entire life is a metaphorical climb to the upper octave, she does not reach it until the moment of death. The locus of the grandmother's "resolution," or final expression of emotion, is the sequence of events leading up to and then following her death—that is, the incidents involved in the famous "Intermittences of the Heart." When the grandmother accompanies Marcel to Balbec, she effectively replaces her daughter in her parental role and, true to the position of self-improvement that she consistently assumes from the beginning of the novel, she first tries to encourage Marcel to break out of his dependency by enjoying the excitement of a new place. It is thus not surprising that she chooses the highest rooms in the hotel ("this belvedere, situated at the very peak of the hotel, that my grandmother had chosen for me," 1.667), perhaps hoping that the walk up to them—like the walk up to the church tower—might give him the strength and perspective necessary to help him control his obsessive resistance to any change.

But it is here that Marcel encounters for the first time an invention that metaphorically signals the doom of the grandmother's hopes for him, an elevator:

> The need I had of my grandmother was heightened by my fear of having caused her a disillusionment. She must be feeling discouraged by the thought that if I couldn't bear this fatigue, then there was no hope that a trip of any sort could ever do me any good. I made up my mind to go back to the room to wait for her; the manager [of the hotel] himself came over to push a button: and a character who was still unknown to me, called the "lift-boy" (who, at the highest point of the hotel, where the lantern in a Norman church would be found, was set up like a photographer behind his curtain or like an organist in his loft), started coming down toward me. (1.664–65)

The "lift-boy" comes down toward Marcel precisely because Marcel, unable to bear his weariness, cannot force himself up the stairs to the rooms that he and his grandmother may indeed be sharing but that they seem to reach, at least metaphorically, in two distinct ways: she by an effort of will and he by taking the easy way, the elevator.[9] That the elevator operator is said to resemble a church organist and the entire trip up to the top of the hotel is compared to a climb to the top of a church reinforces the relation of this passage to the one in which the grandmother looks up admiringly at the church tower singing "an octave above."

It is here that the grandmother seems at last to give up all hope that Marcel will ever be willing or able to make the climb up toward the octave above with her, to follow her up to the heights of self-transcendence through self-resistance. When Marcel begins to bend over to take off his shoes, the grandmother makes an all-important gesture that is a key not only to Marcel's memory of her later on, but also to her identity as Madame Amédée:

> She took such pleasure in any trouble that spared me one, such delight in a moment of stillness and calm for my tired limbs, that when I saw that she wanted to help me lie down [*qu'elle voulait m'aider à me coucher*] and take off my boots and I made the gesture of stopping her [*je fis le geste de l'en empêcher*] and starting to get undressed myself, with a pleading look she stopped my hands, which were touching the first buttons of my jacket and my boots. (1.668)

When Marcel leans over to remove his boots and the grandmother hurries to help him and spare him the effort, she forgoes all of her previous efforts to make him reach up toward the higher level of existence. Let us not forget that when the curé describes the climb up to the top of the church tower for Tante Léonie, he points out that one must bend over to climb up to the top: "on monte plié en deux si on ne veut pas se casser la tête" ("you climb up doubled over to prevent hitting your head") (1.105), *se casser la tête* being a general metaphor for making a great effort. But when Marcel leans over here, it is of course not in order to climb up; on the contrary, he is exhausted even by taking the elevator to the top of the hotel. The grandmother at last gives in and simply helps him undress and go to bed, as one might help a small child: *m'aider à* (*me coucher*) here echoes (even if subconsciously) and replaces *Amédée*. The grandmother no longer tries to prevent Marcel (as she prevented her husband) from being easy on himself. Rather, when he himself makes the empty gesture of mimicking her earlier preventive stances ("je fis le geste de l'en *empêcher*," echoing the grandmother stopping her husband from drinking cognac: "Bathilde! viens donc *empêcher* ton mari de boire du cognac!" 1.11), the grandmother now insists on helping him.

The importance I am placing on this episode may seem exaggerated, but it is in fact to this very scene that Marcel will return when, in the "Intermittences of the Heart," one of the most famous passages in the entire novel, he comes to Balbec a second time and, as he bends over to take off his boots, realizes at last that his grandmother is dead because she is no longer there to help him:

Upheaval of my entire being. On the very first night, as I was suffering from an attack of cardiac fatigue, I bent over slowly and carefully to take off my boots, trying to keep my suffering under control [*tâchant de dompter ma souf-france*]. But I had hardly touched the topmost button of my boot when my chest swelled, filled with an unknown, divine presence, I was racked with sobs, tears streamed from my eyes. The being who answered my calls for help, who rescued me from the dryness of my soul [*la sécheresse de l'âme*], was the same one who, years earlier, at a time of similar distress and loneliness, a time when I had nothing left of myself, had come to my room and given me back to myself.... I had just glimpsed, in my memory, stooped over my fatigue, the tender, preoccupied, disappointed face of my grandmother, just as she had been on that first evening we arrived.... (2.755–56)

It is precisely when Marcel at last follows his grandmother's model and tries to control his suffering ("tâchant de dompter ma souffrance") that he receives the full impact of her death and releases the well of emotion and grief that until now has remained untapped. But what is the meaning of this release of emotion? Is it not the very antithesis of the grandmother's self-restraint, of her own efforts to hide her spiritual and physical suffering from her grandson?[10] How indeed does the grandmother save Marcel from "la sécheresse de l'âme" if she herself systematically refuses to let him see her tears? If in playing Mozart one (correctly) tends to play "drily," how does Madame Amédée go beyond her own "dryness" and thus save Marcel from his?

Love-Death: Reaching the Octave Above

The answer to these questions lies, once again, in the relation between the climb toward the upper octave and the reaching of it. The grandmother may well spend much of her time and energy resisting her feelings, but by resisting them she does not make them disappear; on the contrary, their power and potential never cease to grow. In Proust's universe there is essentially no such thing as getting rid of an obsession or of any powerful feeling; whether one resists one's obsession or not, it is always there, and whether one expresses one's feelings or not, they too persist, even if secretly. What, then, we might ask, is the point in the grandmother's resistance of herself and her feelings?

The climb to the octave above, although it may seem to take place only in space, also occurs through time, and its temporal dimension is one of its key features. Only in the postponement of expression can expression itself—or more specifically the relation between expression and the feelings it expresses—*take on the form of time*. During her life, the grandmother tries to rise above her emotions. At the moment of her death, it is because she has kept all her feelings to herself that their release and expression are experienced as a kind of resolution or rest, a relaxation of the effort involved in climbing the scale. It is because she exists in time, in a constant postponement of expression, that the grandmother actually provides a kind of model for Marcel, for by waiting her entire life to tell her family how much she loves them, she gives the moment of final expression a power that is very much akin to a long-postponed resolution.

Let us look, then, at the grandmother's extremely moving death scene, which culminates in her long-awaited expression of familial love:

> At times it seemed everything was over, the breathing stopped, either by those same changes in octave [*changements d'octaves*] that one hears in the breathing of someone asleep, or by a natural intermittence. . . . Who knows if, even without my grandmother being conscious of it, so many happy and tender states compressed by suffering were not escaping from her now, like those lighter gases that one has repressed for a long time? It seemed that everything she had to tell us was pouring out, that we were the ones she was addressing with this abundance, this urgency, this effusiveness [*cette effusion*]. (2.344)

It is here that the "effusiveness" of the church spire singing an octave above is at last understandable, here that we see why the grandmother enjoys the *potential* of a piano that the church tower might not play drily ("il ne jouerait pas *sec*," which is not to say that it will ever actually play at all). When the grandmother's breathing changes octaves at the moment of death, there is a sense of resolution: she seems to be expressing feelings pent up for many long years. By contrast, the breathing of Tante Léonie, when she *dreams* of Octave, rather than rising an octave, drops down a single tone ("for the music of the snoring was interrupted a second and resumed a tone lower," 1.109). What happens to the grandmother when she reaches the octave above is an expression, in death, of long-resisted love, a resolution that puts an end to the scale. The grandmother has a sort of love-death, and in this very passage we find an extremely important textual variant that will be key to our development: "Wagner, . . . if he ever witnessed a death like this, we may believe that he gleaned from it the inexhaustible repetitions that he eternalized in the death of Isolde" (2.1156–57). The grandmother thus seems to provide an articulation between two musical focuses of Proust's life and his novel: Mozart (Amadeus) and Wagner.[11] In a sense Proust's development is summarized by his change in preference from one to the other, since in the famous questionnaire that he answered as a child he named Mozart as one of his favorite composers, and in a later questionnaire some seven years later that honor goes to Wagner.[12] There is certainly a danger in overschematizing this sort of opposition,[13] and of course I do not mean to imply that Mozart's music is devoid of emotion; rather, I suggest that one might readily associate Mozart and Wagner with two different styles, just as one might identify (at least) two distinct components of Proust's style—an analytical, restrained component and an emotional, expansive one.[14]

Indeed, an issue central to Proust's work is whether it is a novel of analysis that flees and even ridicules all expressions of sentiment, or a novel of thinly veiled emotion; a novel of the head or a novel of the heart. Or, if we consider the relation between the two components of the octave, the climb toward it and the reaching of it, both—that is, a novel whose sustained fear of the power of emotion makes it all the more powerful an expression of emotion. The height of musical stupidity in the *Recherche* is "a noblewoman from Avranches, who wouldn't have been able to distinguish Mozart from Wagner" (2.812). But can we distinguish between what might be called the classical and the romantic elements of this novel? More specifically, what does Proust's musical evolution from Mozart to Wagner mean in terms of the novel?

The importance of this question will not become fully apparent until we focus on the character of Marcel, but let us first look briefly at his worthy precursor in love (as in many other domains), Swann. If Vinteuil's *petite phrase* plays a prominent role in Swann's love for Odette, one of its most important features is its relation to time, and this is immediately apparent in the description of Swann listening to Vinteuil's sonata for the first time:

> But at a certain moment, although he could not make out any clear outline or give a name to what he found pleasing, suddenly enchanted, he had sought to hold onto the phrase or harmony—he didn't know which himself—that was going by and that had broadened his soul. . . . Certainly the notes that we hear at such times already tend . . . to give us impressions of breadth, tenuousness, stability, or capriciousness. But the notes vanish before these sensations are well enough formed in us to escape being submerged by those that the succeeding or even simultaneous notes are already awakening. And this impression would continue to envelop, with its liquidity and its "melting" [*fondu*], the motifs that at certain moments emerge from it, hardly discernible, and then immediately dive back in and disappear, . . . ineffable—if memory, like a worker who toils to establish durable foundations in the midst of the waves, by fashioning for us facsimiles of those fleeting phrases, didn't enable us to compare them to those that follow, and to distinguish them. (1.208–09)

The power of music for Swann lies largely in its relation to time. Even though an infinite potential for evocation seems to reside within each note as it goes by, it is only in the composition, or putting together, of the notes that the true strength of music becomes apparent. The "facsimile" of each note that Swann's memory provides for him is absolutely essential to the experience of music, for it is (literally) the key to the way we perceive the momentum of a musical composition.

Much Western music is based on the principle of tonality, which depends essentially upon two conditions: the establishment of seven tones (out of the available twelve) that form the diatonic scale of a work or a section of a work in a particular key, and the listener's (often subconscious) familiarity with the arrangement of whole and half tones in the major and minor scales. Because of this familiarity the ear can, in certain circumstances, experience a return to the tonic—that is, the tone that establishes the key and is the bottom rung of the scale in that key—as a kind of rest or resolution. As Victor Zuckerkandl puts it: "Hearing music does not mean hearing tones, but hearing, in the tones and through them, the places where they sound in the seven-tone system."[15]

This is exactly how Swann—and although he "doesn't know music" (1.209), he has certainly listened to enough of it to respond to this momentum—is hearing. Music initiates him into a temporally based system, a system that demands the creation of "facsimiles" of notes—or of moments—that can be perceived in relation to other notes or moments. The fact that Swann does not know whether he is hearing a phrase or a harmony—that is, hearing notes successively or simultaneously—shows that every note in a composition based on tonality, whatever its temporal relation to any other note, implicitly retains its position in the scale, whether one hears it relative to others sounded simultaneously or must perceive it in relation to notes that precede and follow it. In fact this is, in part, why music also initiates Swann into the domain of love, Odette being the first woman for whom his feelings go beyond the level of momentary infatuation, the first for whom they develop through time into a complex and gradually evolving system. If Swann's love for Odette is a kind of system—an organization both of the moments he spends with her and of his recollections and anticipations of being with her—then what is new to Swann in this system of love is that its goal is not, as "Un Amour de Swann" makes quite clear, simply "being with Odette," or even the consummation of the relationship. Rather, the goal of this system of love seems to be intimately linked with its temporal dimension, and more specifically with the constant *postponement* of satisfaction, whether it be sexual satisfaction or Swann's ever-increasing (and ever more frustrated) need to feel that he is in possession of every one of Odette's moments.

Postponement, then, is the power of music—and of love—for Swann:

Even this love for a musical phrase seemed for a moment likely to open Swann up to the possibility of a sort of rejuvenation. It had been a long time since he had given up the idea of dedicating his life to an ideal goal and had kept his life within the limits of the pursuit of daily satisfactions. . . . Now, like an invalid who, because of a new place he has been, a different way of life . . . , seems to feel such an improvement in his illness that he begins to imagine the unexpected possibility of starting a new life even after many years, Swann found in himself, in the memory of the phrase he had heard, . . . the presence of one of those invisible realities in which he no longer believed and to which—as if music had had a sort of regenerative influence on his moral dryness [*sécheresse morale*]—he once again felt the desire and almost the strength to consecrate his life. (1.210–11)

Swann's "moral dryness" before he falls in love with Odette makes him quite the opposite of Madame Amédée, she whose outward reserve hides—indeed, constantly replenishes—an inner reservoir of emotion: Swann's dryness is rather an avoidance of love, a refusal to submit to the very form of temporality and postponement that is, as the grand-mother's story so movingly shows, one of love's greatest powers. Music metaphorically takes Swann to "a new place" and "a different way of life"—the very remedies that the loved ones of Marcel and Tante Léonie try to impose on them—and if the *petite phrase* gives Swann a dimension hitherto missing from his life, time, it is precisely because each note, as a part of a dynamic system, embodies the need to go beyond itself in search of a resolution. The *petite phrase* bespeaks the need for a destination, the need to "consecrate one's life" to "an ideal goal." As Zuckerkandl puts it:

A system in which the whole is present and operative in each individual locus, in which each individual locus knows, so to speak, its position in the whole, its relation to a center, must be called a dynamic system. . . . The tones of our tonal system are events in a dynamic field, and each tone, as it sounds, gives expression to the exact constellation of force present at the point in the field at which the tone is situated. Musical tones are conveyors of force. Hearing music means hearing an action of forces.[16]

For the grandmother, "dryness" is merely an outward symptom of an inner effusiveness long postponed; it is neither a negation nor an avoidance, but a dynamic, the sign of a need to wait. This is the musical lesson that Swann in love must learn.

And indeed he does learn it, or at least begins to learn it, through his love for Odette. Early in their relationship, Swann fears that Odette may find him too readily available, and that this is the cause of her "insignificant, monotonous [*monotones*] and apparently unchangeable modes of behavior" (1.225) when they are together. In order to revive her interest he writes to her that he cannot see her, and she responds, terrified of losing him, from the *Maison Dorée* (*do–re*, the names of the first two notes of the solfège scale). Is this slight movement up the musical scale—and let us not forget that Odette's name means "little song"—not an appropriate remedy to the "monotone" into which their relationship is in danger of falling?

Moreover the *Maison Dorée* will take Swann farther up the scale as his love develops. The day he realizes he is in love with Odette is the day he postpones going to see her just a bit too long, misses her at the Verdurins' (1.226), and looks for her in vain at the *Maison Dorée*; when he does finally find her, she claims he simply did not see her there. The coachman who helps him to find Odette is named Rémi (*re–mi*, the second and third notes in the scale) (1.229); here, precisely by postponing his pleasure too long, Swann reaches a new step in the climb up the scale of love, for this is the famous night of the *catleyas*, the night Swann and Odette consummate their relationship.

But in fact this is as far as Swann will climb in the scale of love; he will never make it all the way up to the octave above precisely because his love for Odette, in turn, becomes obsessive and loses the power of resistance and postponement necessary to continue the climb. And it is at this point that Odette sends Swann gently back down the scale of love, first eliminating the *re–mi* step—she tells Swann that he must never take Rémi to come visit her again (1.320–21)—then the *do–re* step—she reveals the fact that she was not at the *Maison Dorée* on the evening of the first night they spent together, but with Forcheville, Swann's rival for her love (1.371), and Swann even suspects that she was with Forcheville when she wrote to him from the *Maison Dorée* (370), which becomes "a cruel name" (372). Swann, pushed back down the scale, does not land on a tonic of resolution, but rather falls back to the monotony of obsession, albeit a different one from the one he experienced at the start: "Swann in Love" moves between Swann's obsessive womanizing (1.191–95) and his obsessive possessiveness, never reaching a resolution. The scale of love stops here.

A(LBERTINE), G(ILBERTE), AND THE TRISTAN CHORD

Let us now turn to the novel's central love story, Marcel's relation with Albertine. In many ways, of course, this liaison echoes Swann's love for Odette, and the equivalent, for Marcel, of Vinteuil's sonata for Swann is Wagner's *Tristan and Isolde*.[17] In *La Prisonnière*, when Marcel is at home waiting for Albertine, he plays a measure of Vinteuil's sonata:

"As I played this measure, . . . I couldn't help murmuring 'Tristan,' with the smile of a family friend who finds something of the grandfather in an intonation or a gesture of the grandson who never knew him. . . . [O]n top of Vinteuil's sonata on the music-stand I installed the score of *Tristan*, fragments of which were being given that very afternoon at a Lamoureux concert" (3.158–59). It is particularly appropriate that "fragments" of *Tristan* are being given at the "Lamoureux" concert (the lover's concert?), for the work itself is about the fragmentary nature of love, its incompleteness so long as it remains in the domain of life, its partiality except in death. The entire scope of Marcel's love life is summarized by the ramifications of this allusion to *Tristan and Isolde*.

Let us recall that already in the description of Marcel's climb up the stairs in Combray, the staircase is described as *triste* and *isolé*, terms that anticipate the French title of Wagner's opera, *Tristan et Iseult*. Marcel climbing the stairs and leaving his mother behind is, like Wagner's hero and heroine, asked to resist an irresistible love. And yet Marcel, even though he never lives up to his grandmother's expectations of him, does follow her model of self-resistance in his own way: after the opening passage that describes the night his mother spends in his room, his obsessive love is displaced, as his sentimental attachments move from his mother to Gilberte, and then finally to Albertine.

It is in fact because the expression of his love for his mother is postponed throughout most of the novel that it has such power when it finally comes in *La Fugitive*. It is only in Venice, after Albertine's death, that Marcel is once again with his mother, and it is possible that a hidden intertext in this sequence may help us to understand the nature of the resolution—or lack of resolution—of Marcel's feelings for his mother that takes place at the end of the Venice episode. I am speaking not of a literary text but rather of a musical text, the prelude to *Tristan and Isolde*. (I might add that Wagner actually wrote a good deal of this opera in Venice;[18] Thomas Mann, in his essay on Wagner, called Venice "the *Tristan* city."[19])

Let us first set the scene in terms of our analysis. The narrator says that in Venice he tastes "impressions analogous to the ones I had so often had in earlier times at Combray, but transposed according to a different and richer mode" (3.623). Many of the questions raised by the Venice passage—and particularly the question of Marcel's relation to his mother—are indeed "analogous" to "Combray"; it is the mode of expression that is different. This "entirely different mode" of Venice is similar to a musical mode, the kind of mode that is inextricably and inexplicably associated with the mood of a musical passage.

One of the "analogies" between Combray and Venice is that Marcel's mother has now assumed the role of her own mother (for whom she is still mourning), and this accounts for her reserved mien:

Mother was reading as she waited for me, her face covered by a tulle veil of a white color that was as heart-rending to me as the color of her hair because I sensed that my mother, hiding her tears, had added it to her straw hat . . . so that she might appear to me to be less in mourning, less sad, almost consoled [*moins triste, presque consolée*]. (3.625)

Marcel's mother seems to be better at doing without her mother than her son was, in Combray, at doing without his. "Hiding her tears," as her mother did throughout her life—and let us not forget that the first adverb applied directly to the grandmother in the novel is *tristement* (1.11), the second adjective *triste* (1.12; the first adjective is *pauvre*)—she appears less *triste*, and, we presume, less *isolée* than Marcel was in the famous scene in Combray, since she seems to draw fortitude from at least pretending to be *consolée*.

Marcel, by contrast, is still *triste* and *isolé*; in the climactic scene of the Venice sequence, when he sits listening to a musician sing "O sole mio" while his mother is on her way to the train station about to leave Venice without him, we find several repetitions of the pairings of *triste* and *isolé* (or *seul*):

Soon she would be gone, I would be alone [*seul*] in Venice, alone with the sadness [*seul avec la tristesse*] of knowing her to be hurt by me, and without her presence to console me [*pour me consoler*]. (3.652)

This diversion, which brought me no pleasure in itself, of listening to *Sole mio*, took on a profound sadness [*tristesse profonde*]. . . . I knew that it meant: "I will be alone [*seul*] in Venice." And perhaps it was this sadness [*cette tristesse*] . . . that caused . . . the desperate but fascinating charm of this song. (3.654)

Triste et isolé, the terms first applied to the staircase that the young Marcel so despairingly climbed at the beginning of "Combray," becomes a kind of refrain in this passage, ultimately indistinguishable from the song "O sole mio" itself, as the *sole* of the title (although it does not mean *seul*) finally comes to be juxtaposed with *tristesse*.

Indeed, the opening notes of another musical composition are operative in this scene as a kind of indicator of its "mode": the beginning of the prelude to *Tristan and Isolde*. The opening measures of *Tristan* are among the most famous in all of Western music: the prelude begins with a minor sixth (A–F), an interval that, to a listener familiar with Wagnerian leitmotifs, instantly evokes an association with unfulfilled longing. This same interval, a minor sixth, is repeated in the first two sung pitches in Wagner's opera (G–E♭); in the solfège scale, the names of these pitches are *sol–mi*. Moreover the word corresponding to the pitches *sol–mi* in Wagner's opera is *Westwärts* ("westwards"), the very direction that Marcel takes in leaving Venice with his mother; and indeed the opening words of the song Marcel is listening to (sol-e mi-o), do seem to be telling him that he must go back whence he came (*Westwärts*), that he can never be without his mother (*isolé* or *seul*) without being *triste*.

What is particularly interesting here is that when the singer reaches the end of his song, he repeats it in a higher register, perhaps an octave above:

> When the phrase was completed down below and the piece seemed to be over, the singer wasn't tired of it and resumed high up as if he needed to proclaim once again my solitude and despair. And out of stupid politeness, as if to show I was being attentive to his music, I said to myself: "I still can't make up my mind; before we decide let's sing the phrase in our head high up." (3.654)

What Marcel wants to gain from listening to "O sole mio" is a "resolution" (the word *résolution* is repeated no fewer than five times in some twenty lines, 3.654); perhaps that is why he sings it again an octave above, hoping for the kind of transcendence and resolution that arriving at the octave can bring.

But in fact the song prevents him from achieving a resolution, and it is here that the opening notes of *Tristan* again become important. The opening measures of the prelude are usually read in the key of A minor, and the first interval, A–F, is followed, after dropping to E, by the so-called Tristan Chord (F–G♯–B–D♯)[20], which some musicologists consider as a kind of modified dominant seventh.[21] If indeed the Tristan Chord is a dominant seventh in the key of A minor, one of the problems it poses is that the dominant seventh is one of the chords that most powerfully demand a resolution. In this case, what seems necessary in order to impart a feeling of resolution from the dominant seventh is an arrival at the octave—that is, a resolution to the tonic. This would confirm the key of the opening bars of the prelude, and would also resolve the tension and anticipation of the dominant seventh, perceptible to even an untrained listener with any familiarity with Western music. As Zuckerkandl puts it:

> The dominant seventh chord is distinguished from all other chords by the fact that its sound makes audible, distinctly and unmistakably, not only a point-beyond-itself but at the same time the goal of that pointing. It strives toward this goal, the tonic chord, ... unmistakably.... In the majority of cases the dominant seventh chord is in fact followed by the tonic.[22]

But in the opening of the *Tristan* prelude, we are not given this tonic resolution.[23] The revolutionary power of this opening is that it refuses to resolve in any expected way:

In the opening measures of the *Tristan* Prelude—probably the most discussed measures in the entire literature of music—the dominant seventh chord suddenly appears, no longer as pointing toward the goal, but as the goal itself! The same chord with which we have been positively forced, by countless repetitions of experience, to associate a particular state, that of concentrated tension immediately *before* the attainment of the goal, now expresses the opposite state, the comparative relaxation of attaining a goal.[24]

The Tristan Chord challenges any traditional notion of resolution, and however one explains these measures theoretically, one would be hard-pressed to think of an opening as searching and unsatisfied as that of the *Tristan* prelude. If the Tristan Chord were followed by the tonic, the G♯ in the chord would resolve to an A. As it is, the passage leaves a feeling of irresolution.

The text of the Venice episode displays a similar lack of resolution. Marcel's running back to his mother at the last moment is the long-awaited expression of emotion that has been displaced and postponed since the heartrending scene in Combray. But in fact that expression of emotion, or resolution, does not come even here; when Marcel jumps onto the train just in time, his mother's reaction echoes the entire Combray drama, but in reverse: "my mother [was] holding herself back in order not to cry, because she thought I wouldn't come" (3.655). It is now the mother who is afraid the son might not come, but she, unlike Marcel as a child, holds back her tears. She, it appears, has inherited from her own mother the ability to resist her emotions, to climb the scale of self-resistance toward the upper octave; she is not yet ready to let out her feelings, to reach a resolution.

But what about Marcel? Is this joining of his mother at the end of "O sole mio" a resolution or a lack of resolution? Our answer appears not in the form of a musical signature but in that of an epistolary signature, in the letter Marcel opens as soon as he is settled on the train with his mother. This is the famous letter from Gilberte announcing her marriage, the letter that gives Marcel an explanation for the earlier telegram he received, supposedly from Albertine, after the latter's death. The mystery of course hinges on the similarity of the two names "Albertine" and "Gilberte"; they are distinguished mainly by the initials *A* and *G* (3.656).[25] Not only are A and G two ends of a scale—indeed, insofar as G♯ is adjacent to the A above it, the proximity of the notes G and A is more obvious than that of the letters—but they are also, in fact, the two notes in the opening of *Tristan and Isolde* that refuse to cooperate: in the prelude, the G♯ refuses to resolve to A, to the tonic.[26]

We are of course dealing with two systems of pitch designation in this chapter, the French solfège *do–re–mi* and the English (and, in a modified form, German) letter names C–D–E (*do* being the equivalent of C in the fixed-*do* system). While the French use the solfège system exclusively, I think it likely that Proust was at least familiar with the Anglo-German system as well. And although it would be difficult to make a claim for Proust's conscious use of the musical scale—in either the solfège or the Anglo-German pitch-name system—he places so much emphasis on the confusion of the *A* and the *G* that I suspect he may have actually been thinking of musical notation here, at least in a general sense. Is there not a feeling in Proust's text that G(ilberte)'s reappearance—which, like a dominant seventh chord, or perhaps a sort of suspension, seems for a time to anticipate the imminent return of A(lbertine)—leaves this climactic moment of Marcel's sentimental life in a state of irresolution?

This is one of the climaxes of Proust's entire novel,[27] for this is the point beyond which Marcel will never fall seriously in love, the triple juncture of his love life that becomes a triple dead end: he leaves behind the prospect of seeing Baroness Putbus's maid, who represents his potential entry into the domain of a Swann-like womanizing (3.651–52); runs after the mother for whom his feelings have clearly never been resolved, and who will never reappear in the novel again once the two arrive home; and then opens a letter on the train that proves at last that Albertine will never return from the dead. If Marcel's love life can be essentially described as a sentimental movement from his mother to Gilberte to Albertine, that movement comes to an end here, with neither a solution nor a resolution.

The Return of Octave

It is perhaps not coincidental, then, given the upper octave's role as a destination, that Marcel later discovers the reason that he lost Albertine is yet another character named Octave, the sportsman from Balbec to whom she was secretly engaged at the time of her death (3.730). This second Octave will in fact allow us, like the structure of the octave itself, both to reach a destination and to return to the beginning—that is, to take one final step that gives us a profound impression of return:

> What struck me in this young man . . . was the extent to which his knowledge of anything involving clothes and how they should be worn, cigars, English drinks, horses, . . . had developed in complete isolation from even the slightest degree of intellectual culture. . . . He could never bear "doing nothing," even though in fact he never did anything. And since complete inactivity ends up yielding the same results as overwork, in the mental realm as well as in the life of the body and the muscles [*la vie du corps et des muscles*], the

steadfast intellectual vacuum that lived inside Octave's contemplative brow had finally given him, in spite of his peaceful appearance, aimless longings for thought that kept him awake at night, as might have happened to an overwrought metaphysician. (3.878–79)

The namesake of Tante Léonie's husband—we are tempted to call him Octave the Second—seems, by his fondness for activity, a worthy heir. The tradition of the o(O)ctave appears to be continued through him, his delight in games and sport a kind of caricature of the first Octave's attempt to get his wife to resist her obsessive inactivity. Since the second Octave is a connoisseur of English drinks, he is undoubtedly an aficionado of tonic, exactly the sort of drink that might do Tante Léonie some good, and in general his concern with muscle tone [*la vie des corps et des muscles*] could provide her with a healthy example.

But in spite of this initial opposition, Octave the Second is ultimately startlingly *like* Tante Léonie: insomniac, overwrought, filled with ill-defined yearnings for something beyond his shallow existence. This is, undoubtedly, an early hint of Octave's future identity as a great artist (3.605–6). Possibly Octave is already beginning to feel here that what he needs is a different kind of tonic: the musical term "tonic." Perhaps what Octave needs is the rest that comes not after a good game of golf (3.878) or a brisk tango (879), but at the end of an exhausting (if rewarding) work of art, whether it be a piece of music that finally resolves to the tonic or a novel that appears at last, after many long pages, to resolve its conflicts.

This dissatisfaction in Octave, this unfulfilled longing for something more, brings us finally to the relation of the octave to the narrator's artistic enterprise. As anyone who has made it all the way to the end of *Le Temps retrouvé* knows, once Marcel returns from Venice the whole question of his own amorous obsessions is eclipsed by his decision to write his novel at last and by the artistic treatise that occupies much of the matinée Guermantes. Proust's novel is, of course, divided into seven parts, which makes *Du côté de chez Swann*—the cycle's starting point and also the point to which it returns—both the novel's tonic and its octave if, at the close of *Le Temps retrouvé*, we have the strength to take the novel's cyclical structure seriously and begin again. But when we start over again, do we feel that the novel in its entirety has in fact resolved anything? Certainly we may be astonished to find that already in the scene of the good-night kiss Marcel's decision to wait up for his mother at any cost is his "resolution" ["je venais de prendre la résolution de ne plus essayer de m'endormir sans avoir revu maman," 1.32]; already Marcel is looking for a resolution, an end to his insomnia, his waiting, his anxiety. But does he reach that resolution by the end of the novel?

Let us not forget that if we have already read the whole novel once, as its structure demands, we are aware of the double identity of this *je*. The *character* Marcel may be searching for a resolution, but the *narrator* has presumably already reached a kind of resolution before he began to tell his story, and it is a resolution not in the sense of determination, but rather in the sense of release and liberation. Insofar as that resolution is a musical gesture, it is not quite so simple as a solution—does a resolution to the tonic really "solve" the tensions in a piece of music?—but rather something like a resignation, an acceptance. What the narrator, then, must understand—just as the second Octave perhaps ultimately understands it—is what happens if one's longings are ever completely fulfilled: death, the final attainment of the octave that puts an end to the climb.

The question then becomes: can one reach the upper octave in anything other than death? Can one capture the experience of the arrival at the tonic—the final expression of one's feelings—in life? The answer for virtually all the characters in Proust's novel is a resounding no. Not only are most of the major characters (and many of the minor ones as well) obsessed by something or someone, but virtually all of them are terrified of ever really revealing their obsession, or even expressing any strong feeling. Vinteuil, desirous but fearful of playing his music when he receives guests, is in this respect not essentially different from Charlus, who has a marked tendency to turn *away* from those who attract him, or from Oriane de Guermantes, who never tells Swann that she is in love with him (although the text makes this plain). Françoise, who mourns Tante Léonie, after the old lady's death, with as much intensity as the two of them spent feuding while she was alive ("in [Françoise there was] a feeling that we had taken for hatred and that was veneration and love," 1.153), is quite similar to Tante Léonie herself, who leaves her fortune to Marcel, "thus revealing after her death an affection for me that I had never suspected while she was alive" (1.454). This is a novel that is at the same time imbued with emotion and resistant to the expression of emotion—which is, of course, one reason why the grandmother is one of its keys, for her story tells us more than anyone's that life is a domain in which one cannot say what one is feeling.

The Last Syncopation

We end, as we began, with the grandmother, the model for the climb to the upper octave and also for its attainment in death. As Proust's own version of a love-death, the text of the grandmother's death is a particularly privileged moment in the narration, and what sets it apart is not only the release of emotion with which it is concomitant, but also, as in the love-death that ends *Tristan and Isolde*, what leads up to it: in this case the grandmother's long preparation for death, which occupies much of *Le Côté de Guermantes*. If we have left this passage for the end and therefore seem to be returning to something that has already been "resolved," this rhythmic postponement follows the model of the grandmother's final illness itself: *la syncope* (2.778; the hotel manager pronounces it *symecope*[28]), which as a medical term means "syncope" (similar to a stroke) and, in the vocabulary of music, "syncopation." Syncopation is, of course, an unexpected irregularity of rhythm, and when Marcel discovers, months after her death, that his grandmother had several syncopes while he was in Balbec with her, he describes his grief with an important musical metaphor:

> So my grandmother had had syncopes and had hidden them from me. Per-haps it had been at the very moment I was being the least kind to her; per-haps she had felt forced, in spite of her suffering, to act cheerful and not get on my nerves, or to pretend to be well so that she wouldn't be made to leave the hotel. "Symecope" was a word that, pronounced in this way, I could never have thought up; if it had been applied to someone else, it might have struck me as ridiculous, but in its strange sonorous novelty [*nouveauté son-ore*], like that of an original discordance [*dissonance originale*], for a long time it remained the single thing that could awaken in me the most painful feel-ings. (2.778–79)

Here, syncopation is a metaphor for the relation between love and the expression of love. In Proust's novel one of the central difficulties of love is the conflict between what the French call *temps forts* and *temps faibles*, strong and weak beats—respectively, moments in which one feels strong emotions and moments in which the general defensiveness and pettiness and even simple reticence of everyday life (and no one portrays these better than Proust) make one fearful about expressing such emotions. When the grandmother has her syncopes, she and Mar-cel are living at two different tempos: his that of the thoughtlessness of everyday life, hers that of the awareness of approaching death. Proustian love is a kind of syncopation precisely because it is an irregularity of tempo, because those who love each other the most, like Marcel and his grandmother, often seem to move at two different tempos or, at the very least, within a single tempo, but at cross-purposes.

This irregularity is, of course, a tremendous source of pain and suf-fering. When Marcel feels the full impact of this "syncope" (in both senses), his pain is described as a "discordance" (*dissonance*), a lack of harmony, a feeling of irresolution. Although his grandmother had her "love-death," Marcel was in one sense unable to hear it until it was too late to respond. But "syncope" is also, by the same token, a potential source of ultimate dignity. It is because life proceeds irregularly, because some things come too quickly and others a bit too slowly, that we are sometimes allowed to live our deaths—that is, to know when death is coming and to begin to experience in life the feeling of resolution that death can bring.

Since the grandmother is the single character whose death is described as a prolonged process that takes place through time—the death of Tante Léonie, by contrast, is nothing more than a parenthesis ("for she had finally died," 1.153)—she would thus appear to have the unique opportunity of expressing her feelings in all consciousness of her imminent death. But as striking as her dignity and courage during this passage is the fact that she does not take advantage of this awareness of death in order to express her feelings; conscious of her imminent death, she never opens up to her loved ones until she loses consciousness (2.344). And indeed, even in the course of her final illness, although now even she is forced to take the elevator (2.317), she continues to ascend a kind of scale, not reaching the top until the moment of death.

The doctors who are called in to treat the grandmother run the gamut in their divergent assessments of the situation. Cottard thinks she is ill but not dying (2.299). Du Boulbon, believing her illness to be imagined (301–7), compares her to Tante Léonie (304) and prescribes brisk walks on the Champs-Elysées (303). Doctor E . . . considers her to be on the brink of death (318). And finally Dieulafoy simply comes as a witness to her death (342). These divergent opinions and diagnoses become a metaphor for all the possible reactions and strategies that any mortal might have in the face of death, whether imminent or not; they are a kind of inventory of the attitudes of the living toward death. The doctors themselves also create a sort of gamut or musical scale through their names, the initials of which "fill in" the scale from A to G: C(ottard), (du) B(oulbon), E . . . , and D(ieula)F(oy), or C, B, E, D, F. Although this name-play seems arbitrary on its own, its relation to the climactic play on A and G in La Prisonnière is suggestive. Is the grandmother, who does in fact provide the articulation between Marcel's relation with Gilberte in Paris and his liaison with Albertine in Balbec,[29] not facing the last scale of her life, preparing herself for the final release?

Of course the grandmother meets these divergent attitudes toward death with her usual aplomb, and if she never achieves a resolution in life, it is precisely because she does not take advantage of this final "syncopation" that life is offering her,[30] the postponement of the time

of her death well beyond the awareness of its inevitability and immi-
nence. It is in this instance that Marcel for the first time goes beyond his
grandmother's example. What allows—indeed forces—the narrator to
begin his novel is the awareness of death. The entire novel is written in
the period of this syncopation, between the awareness of death and
death itself.

To this extent the novel conforms to the double value of the octave.
The first time one reads the novel, it is a climb toward the upper octave—that is, an endlessly postponed emotional expression that climaxes in a nonresolution. But the second time one reads the novel, one
understands for the first time that the novel is in fact not only a climb
toward the upper octave (for Marcel), but also an arrival at the octave
(for the narrator): it, too, is a long-awaited expression of love, not just
(or even especially) for Gilberte or Albertine, or even for Marcel's
mother or grandmother, but rather for every character in the novel. Of
course the narrator's love for his characters is not a simple one: he is
frequently critical of their faults, mocking their manias and obsessions.
But perhaps the overriding and initiating emotion he feels for them—
and even for their manias and obsessions—is love.

It is for this reason that the novel, like the climb up the scale and the
arrival at its upper octave, is both a resistance of emotion and an expression of it. Insofar as the character Marcel is participating, in his
own way, in the ascent up the scale, he is subject to the same inescapable reticence as are all the other characters. But for the narrator, even
though he never quite reaches the resolution of his love story, the
power of the octave comes from one of the most difficult (and important) lessons of human temporality, the double value of death. For if
the final resolution is a release of all of the energy of anticipation that
leads up to it, that resolution is a form of death; but only death—or the
octave above as its analogue—allows one, indeed pushes one, to reveal
at last what one is feeling.

"For what other life was he holding himself back from finally saying
seriously what he thought of things?" (1.98): even this rather cruel
question about Swann becomes a poignant commentary once we realize that it is a rhetorical question, that neither Swann nor any other
character in the novel has any "other life" in which to express himself
and that, nonetheless, in the universe they are inhabiting there is no
possibility for really expressing what they feel. This does not mean that
the narrator is writing from the perspective of knowledge, that by taking pen in hand he shows that he has finally understood his—or
anyone's—life.[31] But it does mean that he is writing from the perspective of love. The entire novel is based on this final, all-encompassing
syncopation linking (or rather separating) a protagonist inhabiting a

temps faible and a narrator positioned in a *temps fort* not of comprehension but of expression. Although the character Marcel is still far from the perspective of love—which is, of course, the perspective of death, the perspective gained from being at the top of the church tower, or from being "perched on living stilts that grow ceaselessly, sometimes becoming higher than church towers (3.1048)—and thus cannot treat the novel's other characters with love, the narrator can—and must—allow himself to portray them with love. He, at last, has reached the octave at the top of the scale.

Chapter 6

MOURNING A MELANCHOLIC:

PROUST AND FREUD ON THE DEATH OF A LOVED ONE

For my grandmother, Anna Becker, in loving memory

PROUST AND FREUD

L ET US NOW approach this same question of the relation between love and death in Proust's novel from a different perspective, a psychological one. Freudian literary criticism has certainly not ignored Proust's novels. Indeed, as J. E. Rivers, author of a recent work entitled *Proust and the Art of Love*, points out, "most of the writing which has been done about Proust's sexuality has been done either from an overtly Freudian perspective or with the Freudian position on human sexuality tacitly taken for granted."[1] In a psychoanalytic study of Proust entitled *Nostalgia*, Milton L. Miller comments that although there appear to be no early, direct links between the work of Proust and that of Freud, "Marcel Proust's intellectual struggles had many parallels with those of Sigmund Freud," and "Proust eventually had a good deal of acquaintance with psychiatry, probably Freudian."[2]

More specifically, Miller is one of several critics to have noticed parallels between certain passages in Proust's cycle of novels and Freud's essay "Mourning and Melancholia," completed in 1915 and published in 1917 and thus coinciding with the period of Proust's life during which he was writing and revising *A la recherche du temps perdu*:

> A great writer in the sphere of mourning, [Proust's] observations were not dissimilar to Freud's and Karl Abraham's on the process of mourning (especially the identification with the deceased, the gradual evolution of comparative indifference through eradication of the beloved image from within oneself, and the mechanisms of delayed mourning reactions in memories, dreams, and symptoms).[3]

Similarly, Randolph Splitter observes that Proust's "penetrating psychological analysis parallels Freud's key text, 'Mourning and Melancholia,' written about the same time, which says that grief is an ambivalent, guilt-ridden identification with the dead in which we 'incorporate' them into ourselves and then gradually, in the process of mourning, give them up again."[4]

My premise in this chapter is that considering Proust's and Freud's texts of mourning together has a synergetic effect: it can yield a definition of mourning that is more complex and and in some ways more satisfying than the conception of mourning depicted by either text on its own. My aim here is not only to try to see how Freud's discussion of mourning can help us to understand certain aspects of Proust's, but also to find out what Proust's text of mourning might itself add to Freud's. As we shall see, when we place these two texts in tandem, each appears to answer a key question left by the other about the process and the stages of mourning.

Once again, as in the preceding chapter, I will focus on Marcel and his grandmother; perhaps this final chapter will consequently create an even stronger impression of déjà vu than the second chapters of each of the preceding sections. But this surface similarity may in fact also give rise to stronger feeling of contrast, as my analysis here will provide a view of the grandmother that appears to be very different from the one suggested in Chapter 5. This is meant to be a tribute to the great complexity and ambiguity of Proust's text, and also to emphasize the capital importance of the different perspectives from which the text invites us to approach it. Let us now turn once again to the relation between love and death in Proust's novel.[5]

MOURNING AND MELANCHOLIA

Let us first look at some of Freud's key statements about mourning and examine what they can tell us about love and self-identity. As James Strachey points out, the three essays "On Narcissism," "Mourning and Melancholia," and "The Ego and the Id" may be taken to form a single thrust developing over the course of a decade; that thrust has to do with the divisions of the human psyche into different functions, and particularly the discovery of a "critical agency" that will lead to the hypothesis of the superego in "The Ego and the Id."[6] Freud in fact distinguishes between mourning and melancholia largely on the basis of this critical agency. He finds that one of the most striking features of melancholia is the impression conveyed by melancholics that what they have lost is less a person they have loved than a sense of their own worth: "In mourning it is the world which has become poor and empty; in melancholia it is the ego itself. The patient represents his ego to us as worthless, incapable of any achievement and morally despicable; he reproaches himself, vilifies himself and expects to be cast out and punished" ("Mourning and Melancholia," 246). Freud goes on to hypothesize that this self-critical capacity—which becomes acutely overdeveloped in melancholics—is actually a part of the normal makeup of the human personality:

> Let us dwell for a moment on the view which the melancholic's disorder affords of the constitution of the human ego. We see how in him one part of the ego sets itself over against the other, judges it critically, and, as it were, takes it as its object. Our suspicion that the critical agency which is here split off from the ego might also show its independence in other circumstances will be confirmed by every further observation. We shall really find grounds for distinguishing this agency from the rest of the ego. What we are here becoming acquainted with is the agency commonly called "conscience"; we shall count it, along with the censorship of consciousness and reality-testing, among the major institutions of the ego. (247)

This critical function, which Freud describes in some detail in this essay,[7] is uncannily applicable to Proust's novel. I am not speaking of the specifically sexual, censuring component of what will later come to be called the superego, which Freud will claim originates in the Oedipal stage as a mechanism prohibiting the realization of desire for the mother,[8] but rather of a more general aspect of the critical function. Those readers of Proust who have the patience to make it through the less famous parts of his work, the central volumes that largely consist of a series of society gatherings observed by the narrator, are likely to be struck by a hyperdeveloped critical agency in the narrator. The humor of many of these passages conceals a criticism that is no less widespread for being generally covert, a criticism that is not, moreover, limited to any particular class of people, but extends to almost every character in the novel, from the maid, Françoise, to the Duchesse de Guermantes.

The view of human nature implicit in the narrator's critical scrutiny is remarkably summed up in Freud's description of the melancholic's critical agency:

> He [the melancholic] seems to us justified in certain other self-accusations; it is merely that he has a keener eye for the truth than other people who are not melancholic. When in his heightened self-criticism he describes himself as petty, egoistic, dishonest, lacking in independence, one whose sole aim has been to hide the weaknesses of his own nature, it may be, so far as we know, that he has come pretty near to understanding himself; we only wonder why a man has to be ill before he can be accessible to a truth of this kind. For there can be no doubt that if anyone holds and expresses to others an opinion of himself such as this (an opinion which Hamlet held both of himself and of everyone else), he is ill, whether he is speaking the truth or whether he is being more or less unfair to himself. ("Mourning and Melancholia," 246–47)

Freud makes use of the literary example of Hamlet to illustrate the illness inherent in the hypercritical agency of melancholia; but the above description of human inadequacy is also an astoundingly accurate encapsulation of almost everything that is wrong with the characters observed by Proust's narrator: "petty, egoistic, dishonest, lacking in independence." Perhaps the most remarkable statement made by Freud in the above passage is this: "we only wonder why a man has to be ill before he can be accessible to a truth of this kind." An overdeveloped critical acuity, whether self-directed or directed toward others, may be incompatible with health even if it is compatible with the truth.

But while Freud opines that Hamlet holds this dismal opinion "both of himself and of everyone else," his entire essay actually hinges on his observations about the relation between self-criticism and criticism of others in melancholia. He goes on to point out that the melancholic's apparent self-criticism is a displacement, that what melancholics are in fact critical of is those they have loved:

> If one listens patiently to a melancholic's many and various self-accusations, one cannot in the end avoid the impression that often the most violent of them are hardly at all applicable to the patient himself, but that with insignificant modifications they do fit someone else, someone whom the patient loves or has loved or should love. Every time one examines the facts this conjecture is confirmed. So we find the key to the clinical picture: we perceive that the self-reproaches are reproaches against a loved object which have been shifted away from it on to the patient's own ego. (248)

What takes the form of self-criticism is covertly dissatisfaction with another, and Freud goes on to outline the process by which this substitution of the object of criticism takes place:

> An object-choice, an attachment of the libido to a particular person, had at one time existed; then, owing to a real slight or disappointment coming from this loved person, the object-relationship was shattered. The result was not the normal one of a withdrawal of the libido from this object and a displacement of it on to a new one, but something different. . . . The object-cathexis . . . was brought to an end. But the free libido was not displaced on to another object; it was withdrawn into the ego . . . [and] served to establish an *identification* of the ego with the abandoned object. Thus the shadow of the object fell upon the ego, and the latter could henceforth be judged by a special agency, as though it were an object, the forsaken object. In this way an object-loss was transformed into an ego-loss and the conflict between the ego and the loved person into a cleavage between the critical activity of the ego and the ego as altered by identification. (249)

I have taken the liberty of quoting this passage at some length not only because it is of great importance to Freud's theory of personality, but also because I believe it to be of particular interest to readers of Proust. As Strachey points out, Freud seems to have considered this description of the process of replacing an object-cathexis by an identification in melancholia to be the most significant aspect of his paper, and Freud later went on to claim a widespread applicability of the process to the formation of character in general.[9] This process of substitution brings up a key question for Proust's narrative: what is the true object of the narrator's critical agency? If in melancholia self-criticism is veiled criticism of others, is the narrator's criticism of others to be construed as covert self-criticism? Certainly Proust's narrator expresses repeated dissatisfaction with the character Marcel, who may be taken to be the narrator's younger counterpart in the novel, but almost always his criticism of Marcel is directed toward the problem of his not beginning to write his book and instead spending his time frequenting the very salons that are themselves a recurrent object of a much more subtle and skillful criticism in the novel. Is the narrator then simply a kind of inverted melancholic, viewing the world with a hypercritical eye that actually sees nothing but his own limitations?

A CASE OF MELANCHOLIA: MARCEL'S GRANDMOTHER

What I would like to suggest is that the narrator's critical point of view can be traced back to the character of Marcel's grandmother. As we saw in Chapter 5, the grandmother is one of the most important characters in the cycle; after the passage dealing with the good-night kiss and the night that Marcel's mother spends in his room, the grandmother virtually replaces her daughter in her affective relations with Marcel. It is she and not his mother who accompanies him to Balbec, she who is repeatedly depicted as caring for him. Moreover her death—including the long illness leading up to it and the even lengthier process of mourning that follows it—is one of the narrative's main events, occupying much of Le Côté de Guermantes and extending into the famous section of Sodome et Gomorrhe entitled "The Intermittences of the Heart," in which Marcel first fully realizes, a full year after her death, that he has lost his grandmother. Largely because of the narrative's dwelling on her death and its aftermath, the grandmother is thus a figure of loss at least equal to Albertine. Since the narrative makes the grandmother's cruciality explicit in the domains of both love and death, it is natural to center a discussion about mourning a loved one on her. But what the novel leaves largely unexplored is the nature of the grandmother's character, and this is an essential element in understanding the relation between Marcel's love of his grandmother and the way he mourns her.

Marcel's grandmother seems to correspond precisely to Freud's description of melancholia, and this is apparent from the first time she appears in the novel:

> Indeed, in order to tease her (she had brought into my father's family such a different turn of mind that everyone poked fun at her and tormented her), since my grandfather was not allowed to drink liqueur, my great-aunt used to give him a few drops. My poor grandmother would come in and fervently beg her husband not to taste the cognac; he would get angry and drink his swallow of cognac anyway, and my grandmother would go back outside, sad, discouraged, but smiling just the same, for she was so humble of heart and so gentle that the tenderness she felt for others and the little heed she paid to herself [*sa propre personne*] and her sufferings joined to give her face a smile in which, quite the opposite of what is visible in the faces of many human beings, there was irony directed only toward herself, and for all of us a kind of kiss, for her eyes could not look at those she held dear without giving them a passionate, caressing look.[10]

Already here the grandmother exhibits certain characteristics suggestive of melancholia. Although she is clearly critical of her husband's shenanigans and disappointed by his disregard for her pleas, her irony is directed only toward herself; what she allows to reach the outer world is only a loving look. Indeed, the grandmother seems to be imitating her husband's attitude toward her when she pays "little heed to herself." Her own person ("sa propre personne") is, by implication, worthless.

If Freud claims melancholia is the result of a disappointment or loss, with what is the grandmother dissatisfied? What has she "lost"? Who or what has let her down? In an immediate sense, the answer to all of these questions is the same: her husband. A strong undercurrent of the long description of Marcel's family life in Combray is the utter particularity of the grandmother and her two sisters, all of whom share a highly developed moral sense and a singular lack of any capacity for humor. The grandfather, by contrast, is more like the family of his son-in-law, Marcel's father: after the grandmother's death, we find out that what differentiates Marcel's mother from her own mother is "her good sense, ... the mocking cheerfulness [*gaîté moqueuse*] that she got from her father" (2.769). This "mocking cheerfulness" might well be considered as evidence of good health; it is paired with "good sense." But from the grandmother's point of view as it is crystallized in the cognac scene, this "mocking cheerfulness" is an endless source of suffering and disappointment—indeed, perhaps the main reason why, when Marcel remembers his grandmother's face at the beginning of the "Intermittences of the Heart," it is "tender, preoccupied and disappointed" (2.756), as if the time since her death had left only her most essential qualities visible.

Only in death is this basic disappointment and disillusionment—the root cause of the grandmother's melancholia—apparent, as we see in this moving description of her as she lies on her deathbed:

> As in the distant past when her parents had chosen a husband for her, her features were delicately etched by purity and submission, her cheeks shining with a chaste hope, a dream of happiness, even an innocent cheerfulness [*innocente gaieté*], which the years had destroyed little by little. The withdrawal of life had just carried away the disillusions of life. (2.345)

Only here are we told that the grandmother's husband was chosen for her by her parents and that she married him out of obedience rather than out of love, and undoubtedly the choice they made was a bad one, for neither her hopes nor her dreams are ever realized. Although she, too, is cheerful as a young girl, her cheerfulness takes such a radically different form—innocence—from that of her husband that it is practically unrecognizable as the same state of mind; even the spelling of the word used here ("innocente *gaieté*") is a variant of the spelling used of the grandfather's cheerfulness ("*gaîté* moqueuse").

This covert object of the grandmother's critical agency becomes generalized into her dissatisfaction with virtually all social life, and it is easy to see how this happens. The childhood drama of the cognac scene contains the germ of one of the issues brought up most repeatedly by Proust's novel, the fundamental cruelty of much social interaction:

> This torture that my great-aunt inflicted on her, the spectacle of my grandmother with her futile prayers and her weakness, beaten before she began, uselessly trying to take the cognac glass away from my grandfather, was one of those things one so gets used to seeing later on that thinking of them makes one laugh, and one sides with the persecutor resolutely and cheerfully [*gaiement*] enough to convince oneself that there is no persecution involved; at the time it gave me such horror that I would gladly have beaten my great-aunt. (1.12)

As a child Marcel identifies with his grandmother and sees the underlying cruelty of the pleasure taken by his grandfather and great-aunt. The narrator implies that as an adult he comes to identify with his grandfather's point of view in this scene and to make light of the unkindness involved. The term *gaiement* prefigures the *gaîté moqueuse* that Marcel's mother inherits from her father rather than the *innocente gaieté* of Marcel's grandmother, for the narrator's position here is anything but naïve. This change in perspective between Marcel and the narrator undoubtedly comes partly from living in society, for this scene is a worthy precursor of the viciousness that characterizes society life in much of the novel, from the Verdurins' salon to the Hôtel de Guermantes. The logical conclusion of this conflict is the grandmother's exclusion from virtually all social life, and this is precisely what happens.

The grandmother's melancholy takes the form of a systematic disillusionment with life in society, a concomitant isolation from everyone except the immediate circle of her family—and an increasing reticence to allow herself any expression of emotion even with them[11]—and an ever-more-exaggerated sublimation of virtually all affection into a love of nature. If she is "always happy to have a pretext to take an extra walk in the garden" (1.14), we come to suspect that this is not only because she loves the garden, but also because she has severe difficulties feeling love for most of the people in the house (apart from Marcel and his mother, of course). She is undoubtedly the only person who goes to Balbec to look at the scenery rather than at the people: "My grandmother . . . thought that at the seaside one must be on the beach from sunrise to sunset breathing in the salt and that one must know no one, because visits and trips are that much time taken away from the sea air." (1.129–30)

The grandmother's unwillingness to have an active social life is inextricably bound up with the two main features of melancholia as Freud describes them: dissatisfaction with others—in this case encapsulated by the grandmother's "loss" (that is, refusal) of her husband as a suitable partner—and the resistance to giving voice to one's dissatisfaction—which leads the grandmother to displace her severity and discontent onto herself. It is true that the grandmother is not openly critical either of herself or of others, unlike Freud's melancholics, who revel in their self-criticism precisely because it is actually criticism of others. But despite the internalization of her critical function, there is still a strong suggestion that she shifts her dissatisfaction with others onto herself, and this is already visible in the novel's first description of her.

In this passage near the beginning of "Combray," the grandmother is seen walking alone in the garden in the midst of a cloudburst, so preoccupied by her thoughts that she lets her skirt get covered with mud:

> She would say, "Finally you can breathe!" and walk along the rain-soaked paths—to her way of thinking too symmetrically lined up by the new gardener who was lacking in feeling for nature [du sentiment de la nature] . . . — with her little enthusiastic and jerky step, keeping pace with the various movements excited in her soul by the intoxication of the storm, the power of hygiene, the stupidity of my education, and the symmetry of the gardens, rather than with the wish—unfamiliar to her—of keeping her plum-colored

skirt free of the mud stains under which it disappeared up to a height that was always a problem and a source of despair for her chambermaid. (1.11)

The grandmother's emotions—the "various movements" of her soul—are not directed outward, toward those who are their actual object. Rather, they simply power her solitary walk, as the speed of her steps is determined by these internal motions. Indeed, none of the human objects of her emotions are actually identified, although it is increasingly clear who those objects would be: the intoxication of the storm is the only emotion with no personal object, a solitary enjoyment, and while the power of hygiene may be quite general it already hints at the sickly Marcel and his overindulgent parents. "The stupidity of my education" makes that suggestion explicit, and the symmetry of the gardens can easily be blamed on the previously-mentioned gardener. The feeling that this ill-chosen gardener lacks is the very emotion into which much of the grandmother's own sentimental life is sublimated, a "feeling for nature" ("sentiment de la nature").

As striking as the narrative's reticence—presumably mimicking the grandmother's—to name the objects of her feelings of dissatisfaction and thus to give voice to open criticism of others is the grandmother's own willingness—one might almost say eagerness—to allow herself to be covered with mud. This then becomes a metaphor for the displacement of any potential "mudslinging" that the grandmother might feel tempted to do if she spoke her criticisms aloud: rather than sullying anyone else's good appearance, she redirects her criticisms inward and fairly disappears under a wall of mud. When the chambermaid despairs of ever getting her mistress's plum-colored skirt—yet another indication of her *penchant* for nature—clean, we are being told of the incompatibility of the grandmother's melancholia with life in society.

NARCISSISM AND MELANCHOLIA

But the grandmother's aversion to social interaction because of her melancholia is what strengthens her relation to Marcel, for her melancholia is not completely separable from the nurturing role she plays for her grandson. Not only does the antisocial aspect of her melancholia free her from other attachments, but the selflessness it fosters makes her precisely the kind of all-giving figure Marcel needs. As Freud points out, "another person's narcissism has a great attraction for those who have renounced part of their own narcissism and are in search of object-love" ("On Narcissism: An Introduction," 14.89). It would be only slightly simplifying the bond of affection linking the grandmother to Marcel to say that her melancholia and his narcissism enter into a symbiotic relation, each finding its needs fulfilled by the other.

The narrator repeatedly makes clear that Marcel feels his grandmother exists only for him. Her utter availability to him is particularly important by contrast to Marcel's mother, who is openly attached to her husband, her time divided between him and Marcel.[12] This is obvious even as early as the section dealing with the good-night kiss, but the fact that the conjugal relation takes precedence over the maternal one is most effectively suggested when Marcel is separated from his mother for the first time: "For the first time I felt that it was possible for my mother to live without me, to live otherwise than for me, with another life. She was going to live apart, with my father, whose own existence she probably thought was somewhat complicated and saddened by my bad health and my nervousness" (1.648). While Marcel's grandmother goes with him to Balbec for a prolonged stay, his mother and father go off to a place with a particularly suggestive name:

> It was with a heavy heart that I looked at her [my mother] as if she were already separated from me, wearing the straw hat she had bought for her stay in the country and the light dress she had put on because of the long trip in the heat. They made her look different, as if she already belonged to the villa of "Montretout," where I would not see her. (1.651)

The villa of "Montretout," or "Show-all," is the place where the mother will "show everything" to her husband and not to Marcel who, in spite of his mother's light dress, cannot see what his father will see: "the villa of 'Montretout,' where I would not see her."

It is in this context that the grandmother's complete devotion to Marcel assumes its full value. Unless one pays very close attention to certain chronological details, one can very easily get the impression that the grandmother is a widow, and that this partly accounts for her availability to Marcel. But in fact Marcel's grandfather is present at his wife's bedside at the moment of her death (2.341–44). We can only conclude that her prolonged stay in Balbec with Marcel and without her husband—who is not mentioned even once during the entire visit to Balbec—represents no hardship to her, which should not surprise us given what we know about her rejection of him. She, unlike her daughter, is able to commit herself fully to Marcel.

The picture of the grandmother painted by the narrator is thus of a being without any self-regard, a being who exists only for Marcel:

> [Hers was] a love in which everything found its complement, its goal, its constant direction in me, to such an extent that all the geniuses who had existed since the beginning of the world would not, in my grandmother's eyes, have been worth a single one of my faults. (2.758)

She was my grandmother and I was her grandson. The expressions on her face seemed to be written in a language that was only for me; she was everything in my life, the others existed only relative to her, to the judgment she would give me of them . . . (2.775)

One might think the only thing that could separate Marcel and his grandmother would be death, but it is precisely at the two moments when he most feels the impact of her death—when hearing her voice on the telephone for the first time prefigures her death and when he at last realizes in the "Intermittences of the Heart" that she is dead—that the nature of his attachment to her is clearest. Unlike the case of his mother, being apart from his grandmother only emphasizes their inseparability:

[Her voice on the telephone] was gentle, but also how sad it was, most of all because of its very gentleness, removed—more than most human voices have ever been—from any harshness, from any element of resistance to others, from any selfishness [*égoïsme*]! (2.135)

The being who answered my calls for help, who rescued me from the dryness of my soul, was the same one who, years earlier, at a time of similar distress and loneliness, a time when I had nothing left of myself, had come to my room and given me back to myself, for she was myself and more than myself. (2.755–56)

The grandmother *is* Marcel: at the same time that her melancholia makes her feel that she is nothing without him, his narcissistic needs make him feel that he is nothing without her.

Perhaps the apogee of this *folie à deux* comes, appropriately, in the narrator's memory of losing his grandmother as a child: "I shook with the same anguish I had once felt long, long ago, on a day when, as a small child, I had lost her in a crowd; not so much the anguish of perhaps not finding her again as the anguish of feeling that she was looking for me, of feeling that she was telling herself that I was looking for her" (1.136). What is being described here is a circle of projections. Marcel's anguish comes not from losing his grandmother, nor even from thinking that she is anxious at having lost him, but rather from imagining that she is anxious at the thought that he is looking for her. This is a double projection that boomerangs back onto Marcel: he first puts himself in his grandmother's place in wondering how she is feeling, but once he finds himself in that place he then immediately reprojects himself—that is to say, his grandmother, in whose place he is standing—back into his own place. Losing his grandmother does not lead to a state of independence or even of separability from her, but rather exacerbates the confusion of their identities.

THE HERITAGE OF MELANCHOLIA

It is thus not surprising that the confusion of Marcel's identity and his grandmother's goes even further when he loses her as an adult, at the time of her death—or, more precisely, when he finally understands that he has lost her in the "Intermittences of the Heart." It is largely this confusion that makes Marcel's initial reaction to his loss a form of melancholia rather than mourning, for his loss first appears as an ego-loss rather than an object-loss.

Marcel blames himself for his grandmother's death. Quite aside from the fact that in the terms of the narration his last kiss seems to precipitate her death (2.344–45), learning all the details of her illness months after her death makes him feel responsible for it. When the director of the Grand Hotel in Balbec tells Marcel that his grandmother had "symecopes"—a mispronunciation of the medical term "syncope," a kind of stroke—long before Marcel realized it, the mispronounced word "symecope" seems to carry a secret message of guilt:

> So my grandmother had had syncopes and had hidden them from me. Perhaps it had been at the very moment I was being the least kind to her; perhaps she had felt forced, in spite of her suffering, to act cheerful and not get on my nerves, or to pretend to be well so that she wouldn't be made to leave the hotel. "Symecope" was a word that, pronounced in this way, I could never have thought up; if it had been applied to someone else, it might have struck me as ridiculous, but . . . for a long time it remained the single thing that could [*était capable*] awaken in me the most painful feelings. (2.778–79)

The syllable added to the word *syncope*, "-me," undoubtedly suggests Marcel's unresolved feelings of responsibility and guilt over his selfish treatment of his grandmother, his inability to perceive her illness and to treat her as anything other than someone whose function in life was to satisfy his needs. The word's final syllable, "-cope," may even suggest the Latin *culpa*, "guilt," hence the French *coupable* (the latter term being further hinted at by the phonetically similar adjective *capable* applied to the word *symecope*). In *symecope*, then, Marcel might well hear *mea culpa*, and it is perhaps for this reason that the word stirs up such painful feelings in him: the source of his suffering is not simply the loss of his grandmother, caused by a syncope, but rather what he perceives as his own role in that loss.

Another, equally compelling example of Marcel's implication in his grandmother's death has to do with the photograph that she has taken of herself when she discovers she is seriously ill. Not understanding the real reason for the portrait and attributing it to what he imagines to be the grandmother's own narcissism, Marcel torments her much more cruelly than his grandfather and great-aunt at Combray:

My only conceivable happiness now [after the grandmother's death] resided in being able to find happiness spread across the remembered surfaces of her face, molded and sloped by tenderness, but in earlier times I had put an insane fury into my efforts to eradicate her slightest pleasures, like the day Saint-Loup had taken grandmother's picture and I had been unable to contain how childish and almost laughable I found the coquetry of her pose, with her wide-brimmed hat, in a flattering half-light. I had gone so far as to murmur a few impatient, injurious words that—I had felt it by a contraction of her face—had struck home, had hurt her; I was the one they were tearing apart now that I could no longer console her with a thousand kisses. (2.758–59)

This scene shows not only the unremitting nature of Marcel's narcissistic attachment to his grandmother while she was alive, but also his identification with her after her death. The single thing most capable of pushing Marcel to cruelty toward his grandmother is the possibility that she—whose selflessness is at the very core of her relation with him—might herself have the potential for narcissism. For it is to narcissism—undoubtedly the projection of his own rampant narcissism in his relation to her—that Marcel attributes her desire for a flattering portrait, although as he will soon find out her real concern was to conceal her illness from her family (2.776).

At least as important as this symbiotic relation between Marcel's narcissism and his grandmother's selflessness is his identification with her after her death. The pain he inflicted upon her becomes his own pain ("I was the one they were tearing apart"), as it is deflected away from the lost love-object and redirected back toward the image of the love-object that the ego has now internalized in reaction to its loss. The proof that Marcel has started to become his grandmother is that his attitude toward his memory of her essentially duplicates her general attitude toward him: his "only conceivable happiness" consists of finding happiness in his grandmother's face as he remembers it. Marcel's indifference (not to say downright hostility) to his grandmother's happiness in life, apparent in the incident of the photograph, becomes reversed into an obsessive concern for her happiness and a rejection of his own once she has died.

MOURNING A MELANCHOLIC

Does this mean that Marcel mourns his grandmother, who was herself a melancholic, by becoming a melancholic? But if in Freud's discussion melancholia is an alternative to mourning rather than a form of mourning, how can one mourn someone—even a melancholic—by becoming a melancholic?

In fact Marcel's reaction to his loss goes beyond melancholia, and Proust's text gives us a picture of mourning that, although it is in some respects extraordinarily close to Freud's, has its own remarkable, distinctive features. And it is both this closeness and this distinctness that allow the two visions of mourning to illuminate each other. Let us first look at how the process of mourning that takes place in the "Intermittences of the Heart" resembles Freud's depiction of mourning.

The process Marcel goes through begins with melancholia and then moves on to mourning (and even, as we shall see, to something beyond mourning as Freud describes it). Marcel's initial reaction is an impression of ego-loss very much like that described by Freud: it is characterized by a lowering of self-esteem (feelings of guilt), a loss of interest in all activity (Marcel spends his time in his room and refuses all contacts) and the inability to love (he sends Albertine away without seeing her). Unlike the process of mourning, in which "reality-testing has shown that the loved object no longer exists" ("Mourning and Melancholia," 244), the emotional phase Marcel first goes through places reality only in the being who has been lost:

> While my mother read on the beach I stayed in my room, alone. I remembered the last times of my grandmother's life and everything that had to do with them, the stairway door that was held open when we went out for her last walk. By contrast to all of that, the rest of the world seemed hardly real [à peine réel] and my suffering poisoned it completely. (2.772)

Whereas in mourning, reality-testing teaches the mourner—however slowly and painfully—that reality lies with the world from which the lost loved one is now absent, here Marcel's only reality resides in the minutest memories of his grandmother: the rest of the world is "à peine réel."

But Marcel does eventually move on to the work of mourning. What started out as a pure ego-loss becomes an object-loss, an impoverishment of the world from which the grandmother has been taken away. This becomes clear in the final long paragraph of the "Intermittences of the Heart" (2.780–81), which I will try to demonstrate is one of the most important passages in the entire Recherche. In this paragraph Marcel finally decides to see Albertine again, and after she leaves to go home, he takes a walk along the path on which he and his grandmother so often rode with Madame de Villeparisis. There he sees the apple trees in full blossom, a sight that he and his grandmother never saw together. Under a changing sky, he watches as the clear weather gives way to a cloudburst, and the section (and the entire chapter of some 150 pages) ends with the apparently simple phrase: "it was a spring day" [*c'était une journée de printemps*].

What pulls Marcel out of his melancholia and allows him to begin the work of mourning is the possibility of new pleasures, precisely as Freud observes:

Each single one of the memories and situations of expectancy which demonstrate the libido's attachment to the lost object is met by the verdict of reality that the object no longer exists; and the ego, confronted as it were with the question whether it shall share this fate, is persuaded by the sum of the narcissistic satisfactions it derives from being alive to sever its attachment to the object that has been abolished. ("Mourning and Melancholia," 255)

The process of mourning has begun—and perhaps, in keeping with the "intermittency" of virtually all perception of emotion in Proust, has even already made a good deal of progress—when Marcel allows himself to take pleasure in seeing something his grandmother never saw, the flowering of the apple trees in Balbec. What draws him away from his obsession with his grandmother is "the thousand cries of the children playing, of the swimmers joking with each other, of the newspaper vendors" (2.780); it is to Marcel himself that they are calling out with the possibilities of youth, pleasure, and new things.

Moreover we may safely presume they have been calling out during the entire time Marcel has been at Balbec; why, then, can he hear them only now? While the passage does not explicitly tell us the reason, its structure strongly suggests that what allows Marcel to mourn his grandmother is the passage of time:

Then one day, I made up my mind [*Puis un jour, je me décidai*] to send Albertine a message saying that I would receive her presently. It was . . . a day of premature sweltering heat . . . (780)

Then [*Puis*] the rays of the sun were suddenly followed by those of the rain. . . . it was a spring day. (781)

This final paragraph is more or less set off by the word *puis*, which is normally simply indicative of a succession but here has an element of causality. The paragraph's opening phrases, "Puis un jour, je me décidai" are tantamount to cause and effect: when enough time has passed, Marcel makes up his mind to live for something other than the loss of his grandmother. Like the weather on a spring day, Marcel here reveals a capacity for change.

In a sense this is where the process of mourning as Freud describes it in "Mourning and Melancholia" ends: Marcel has detached himself from his grandmother to a great enough extent to form other emotional cathexes and to take pleasure in things unrelated to the lost loved one.

Freud certainly does not make light of the difficulties and the efforts involved in the process of mourning, nor does he say that it is necessarily a short process; the demands that reality-testing makes upon the mourner to return to life "are carried out bit by bit, at great expense of time and cathectic energy, and in the meantime the existence of the lost object is psychically prolonged" ("Mourning and Melancholia," 245). But in mourning as Freud describes it, the process has fairly clear boundaries: it ends, more or less, when the mourner has detached him- or herself from the lost object of affection and shifted cathectic energy onto others.

Freud himself seems to have been somewhat unsatisfied with this vision of the end of mourning. He supposes that when mourning "has run its course," the reason that there is no "phase of triumph" is that the "work of severance is so slow and gradual that by the time it has been finished the expenditure of energy necessary for it is also dissipated" ("Mourning and Melancholia," 255). But he is disturbed by this lack of "triumph"; perhaps he senses that the process of mourning as he describes it seems incomplete. He wonders why the ego is so strongly resistant to mourning, why it has such pain and difficulty detaching itself from a lost object when in many cases other potential love-objects are close at hand:

> Why this compromise by which the command of reality is carried out piecemeal should be so extraordinarily painful is not at all easy to explain in terms of economics. It is remarkable that this painful unpleasure is taken as a matter of course by us. The fact is, however, that when the work of mourning is completed the ego becomes free and uninhibited again. ("Mourning and Melancholia," 245)

Is the ego really "free and uninhibited" when mourning is over? Does the loss of a loved one call for nothing more than detachment? Is mourning then devoid of any special form of closure? And without such a closure, is mourning not essentially an entropic process of a progressive loss of energy, one that ends with a whimper rather than with a bang?

Proust's text seems to take the process of mourning one step further than Freud's essay by addressing these questions, for what punctuates Marcel's mourning of his grandmother is not simply a detachment, a withdrawal of emotion. Proust's text, with its vision of "intermittent" temporality, tells us that the process of mourning not only cannot be regularized, but also that in some respects it *cannot come to an end*. The fact that even after Marcel has moved on to the work of mourning his grandmother he will not simply detach himself from her is suggested by the vicissitudes of the weather here: the day begins as a foretaste of summer and ends with a memory of winter, with a "wind turned icy" (781). This is precisely what makes it an archetypal "spring day," for in Proust time itself, and not just the human heart, essentially moves by "intermittences," unevenly pulled between the past and the future.

What Proust tells us more generally is that the ongoing mourning of a loved one consists of paying tribute to the person whom one has lost by incorporating that person's perspective on the world into one's own. This longer-term stage of mourning begins to take place in the final paragraph of the "Intermittences of the Heart":

> I went off alone to take a walk along that wide road that Madame de Ville-parisis's carriage used to follow when we took rides with my grandmother; pools of water, which the brilliant sunshine had not dried up, made the earth into a veritable swamp, and I thought of my grandmother who in earlier days couldn't take two steps without getting dirt on herself. (781)

This is, significantly, Marcel's first memory of his grandmother since he began mourning her death that has nothing to do with either her death or the period leading up to it. It is, if we recall the beginning of "Combray," a memory of the characteristic pose in which we first see her as she strolls through the rain-soaked garden and takes no notice of the dirt she is getting on her skirt. The grandmother covered in mud becomes an implicit model—or rather countermodel—for all life in society, and it is as such that Marcel begins to internalize his grandmother's point of view:

> But, as soon as I had reached the road, what a dazzling sight! In the very place where with my grandmother in the month of August I had seen nothing but the leaves or the location of the apple trees, as far as the eye could see they were in full flower, shockingly luxuriant, their feet in the mud and dressed up for a formal ball [*en toilette de bal*], taking no precautions to avoid ruining the most marvelous pink satin that had ever been seen and that gleamed in the sunlight. (781)

One of the central metaphors of Proust's cycle is "young girls as flowers," a metaphor that the title of the second novel, *A l'ombre des jeunes filles en fleurs*, emphasizes by the puzzling plural *fleurs*; if the girls were simply *in flower*, the singular *fleur* would be more usual. "Les jeunes filles en fleurs," then, are girls *as* flowers, as in the common construction "être habillé en . . ." ("to be dressed as . . ."). In this passage we might at first have the impression that the metaphor is simply reversed: the flowers, veritable *fleurs en jeunes filles*, are dressed as young girls going to a ball.

But there is something more here, something crucial to the narrator's assumption of his grandmother's perspective. Albertine and her friends might be carefree and even careless while gamboling on the beach, but it is doubtful they would be willing to let pink satin dresses get covered with mud before a formal dance. Why then, when Marcel looks at these flowering trees, does he see them muddying their fine clothes?

The model for the negligent apple trees is, of course, Marcel's grandmother, and this forces us to correct the metaphor being established here in two ways—by changing young to old and plural back to what is now an unexpected singular: "des fleurs en vieille dame," or flowers imitating an old lady. This reversed metaphor is one of the keys to the narrator's observations of society. The impression given by these observations is, as we have seen, that virtually everyone in society seems ridiculous, pretentious, and contrived—in short, the opposite of the grandmother, who is dignified, humble, and natural. But what this passage shows us is that the narrator's observations are less a criticism of a series of individuals—some of whom actually lose much of their falseness when seen outside of society—than a fundamental and overwhelming dissatisfaction with all social life, which is precisely Marcel's inheritance from his grandmother. Marcel lives in society, which his grandmother refused to do, but he observes it *from her perspective*, through her disappointment with the cruelty and the pettiness of the world. Marcel's homage to his grandmother—what survives his detachment from her and makes mourning her into an ongoing process— is that he implicitly judges the world (and, as we might well expect, judges it harshly) through her eyes. Thus if there is an almost constant, merciless irony in the narrator's accounts of society life, there is no properly social position from which the irony is directed, but rather only the (implicit) solitary position of the grandmother. This homage that the narrator pays to the grandmother is like the mourner's acknowledgment of his heritage. It says that even after what Freud would call the work of mourning has taken place, one can never—and must never—let the loved one go.

MOURNING PROUST

I have tried to show that this is the way Proust's text of mourning goes a step further than Freud's and, by the same token, answers a question that is at least hinted at by Freud's essay. But in conclusion I would like to suggest that Proust's text in fact does nothing more than anticipate— unintentionally, we must presume—what Freud himself will conclude several years after the publication of "Mourning and Melancholia." Here is a passage taken from "The Ego and the Id" (1923):

When it happens that a person has to give up a sexual object, there quite often ensues an alteration of his ego which can only be described as a setting up of the object inside the ego, as it occurs in melancholia; the exact nature of this substitution is as yet unknown to us. It may be that by this introjection, which is a kind of regression to the mechanism of the oral phase, the ego makes it easier for the object to be given up or renders that process possible. It may be that this identification is the sole condition under which the id can give up its objects. At any rate the process, especially in the early phases of development, is a very frequent one, and it makes it possible to suppose that the character of the ego is a precipitate of abandoned object-cathexes and that it contains the history of those object-choices. ("The Ego and the Id," 19.29)

Freud here recognizes that *even for a nonmelancholic*, the giving up of a loved one leaves the same sorts of traces that are found in cases of melancholia. Character itself is "a precipitate of abandoned object-cathexes," and "contains the history of those object-choices."

Even if Freud was wholly unaware of Proust's work in 1923, the year "The Ego and the Id" appeared, this text, which came out a few short months after Proust's death, seems like an unconscious tribute to Proust, an assertion similar to what Proust himself had been trying to say about mourning. The observation Freud makes in the year after Proust's death is like a kind of mourning of the French master of love, loss, and mourning, an espousal of his perspective. What Freud seems to be saying is that, far from being able to replace what we have lost, we become what we have lost, or more specifically we become what we have loved and lost. A simpler and more complex conclusion about mourning can hardly be imagined, nor one that comes closer to capturing the spirit of *A la recherche du temps perdu*.

NOTES

INTRODUCTION

1. For an interesting discussion of this question, see Maurice Blanchot, *Le Livre à venir* (Paris: Gallimard, 1959), 18–34, esp. 22–23.

2. Antoine Compagnon, *Proust entre deux siècles* (Paris: Seuil, 1989), 10. This and all translations from the French, unless otherwise noted, are my own.

3. Gérard Genette goes so far as to say that the entire cycle of novels seems to "swell out" (*se gonfler*) from an "embryonic" passage of no more than seven pages written in 1909. "La Question de l'écriture," in Roland Barthes et al., *Recherche de Proust* (Paris: Seuil, 1980), 8.

4. Compagnon, *Proust entre deux siècles*, 50.

5. The instability and ambivalence of the novel's conclusion are reflected by the change of title that the final volume underwent. Proust originally thought it would be called *Adoration perpétuelle*, a title that underscores the narrator's search for immortality and the eternal. As Proust himself recognized in speaking to his friend Jacques Benoist-Méchin shortly before his death, the change in title to the much less affirmative *Le Temps retrouvé* was a virtual admission of defeat. Whether or not we consider the phenomenon of excessive digression to be one of the causes of the change in valence of the cycle's ending, the fact remains that the possibility of transcending the world of the narrative through its ending became more and more remote at the same time that the novel's original form was being distended almost beyond recognition by insertions.

6. Quoted in Walter Benjamin, *Illuminations*, trans. Harry Zohn (New York: Schocken, 1969), 204.

7. Paul Valéry, "Hommage à Marcel Proust," in *Oeuvres*, 2 vols. (Paris: Gallimard, Pléiade, 1957–1960), 1.771. Originally published in *La Nouvelle Revue Française* 112 (1 January 1923), an issue devoted to Proust shortly after his death.

8. T. S. Eliot, *The Sacred Wood* (1920. Reprint. London: Methuen, 1969), 49–50.

9. Roland Barthes, *Le Plaisir du texte* (Paris: Seuil, 1973), 59.

10. Benjamin, *Illuminations*, 205.

CHAPTER 1

1. Peter Brooks, *Reading for the Plot: Design and Intention in Narrative* (New York: Alfred A. Knopf, 1984), 63.

2. See Gérard Genette, *Figures III* (Paris: Seuil, 1972), 182.

3. I am forced to use this term for lack of a better one, although it has several disadvantages. First, I do not intend the term to be gender-specific, but rather to refer to both aunts and uncles. Second, the term "avuncular" has moral overtones that suggest a protective relationship of spiritual guidance, whereas in Proust it has quite a different moral resonance.

4. See also Janet Beizer, *Family Plots* (New Haven: Yale University Press, 1986), particularly Chapter 3, "Mirrors and Fatherhood: Le Père Goriot," 103–39. Peter Brooks points out that in the Romantic tradition the theme of fraternal and sororal incest represents the temptation of nonnarrative, "the very cessation of narrative movement" (Brooks, *Reading for the Plot*, 109).

5. Edward W. Said, *Beginnings: Intention and Method* (New York: Basic Books, 1975), 66.

6. Marcel Proust, *A la recherche du temps perdu*, ed. Pierre Clarac and André Ferré (Paris: Gallimard, Pléiade, 1954), 1.773. All quotations of Proust's novel will be taken from this edition, and subsequent references will be given in the body of the text. All English translations of Proust and other French texts are my own.

7. In my general approach to this question of narrative and familial axes I am influenced by the parallels that Claude Lévi-Strauss makes between linguistic structures and kinship structures. See, for example, the section "Langage et parenté" in *Anthropologie structurale* (Paris: Plon, 1958), 35–110.

8. There is of course an extremely important nonvertical familial link made in the *Odyssey* as well, Odysseus's reunion with Penelope, although it is not a fraternal or sororal link but rather a conjugal one.

9. Homer, *Odyssey*, ed. Thomas W. Allen (1908. Reprint. Oxford: Clarendon Press, 1966), Book 16, lines 117–20. All references to Homer will be to this edition, and book and line numbers will subsequently be given in the body of the text. Translations of Homer are my own.

10. Bennett Simon, "The Hero as an Only Child: An Unconscious Fantasy Structuring Homer's *Odyssey*," in *International Journal of Psychoanalysis* 55 (1974): 560. This paucity of siblings in the *Odyssey* becomes even more striking by contrast with the *Iliad*, which is almost completely organized around brotherly and sisterly relationships (Menelaos and Agamemnon, Hector and Paris and their forty-eight brothers and numerous sisters, Helen and Clytemnestra, etc.). As W. B. Stanford points out, Odysseus is the only major figure in the *Iliad* who has no brother or close companion. See *The Ulysses Theme: A Study in the Adaptability of a Traditional Hero*, 2d ed. (Ann Arbor: University of Michigan Press, 1976), 43–44.

11. The link between storytelling and paternity is made by Roland Barthes: "The death of the Father will take away from literature many of its pleasures. If there is no more Father, what is the good of telling stories?" *Le plaisir du texte* (Paris: Seuil, 1973), 75. "It may be significant that at the same time (around the age of three) human offspring 'invent' the sentence, narrative, and the Oedipus complex." "Introduction à l'analyse structurale des récits," in *Communications* 8 (1966): 27.

12. Aunt Léonie is actually not Marcel's aunt but rather a fairly distant cousin. Nonetheless she is always identified as "tante Léonie" or "ma tante Léonie."

13. From this point of view it is instructive to contrast Aunt Léonie's death, which is reported practically as an aside ("for she had finally died," 1.153), to the grandmother's illness and death and the family's mourning of her, all of

which stretch out over hundreds of pages in *Le Côté de Guermantes* and *Sodome et Gomorrhe*.

14. For a more general discussion of lying and truth in the novel, see René Girard, *Mensonge romantique et vérité romanesque* (Paris: Grasset, 1961).

15. I would argue that Odysseus's paternity, his place in the family lineage, is at least as important a factor in his need to return home in spite of the various temptations he encounters along the way as his desire to be reunited with Penelope. The narrative itself suggests this by making Odysseus's temptations all take the form of potential marriage partners rather than that of surrogate children, which is certainly theoretically possible (cf. Telemachos's attachment to the father figure of Eumaios, the swineherd).

16. As Roman Jakobson puts it: "There are two Odysseuses in the *Odyssey*: one who has adventures, another who tells about them. It is difficult to say which of the two is the main character." *Poétique de la prose* (Paris: Seuil, 1971), 75.

17. I believe it is not coincidental that Proust's literary executors have been his niece, Suzy Mante-Proust, and now his great-grandniece, Nathalie Mauriac, who co-edited the recently discovered and published deathbed revisions of *Albertine disparue* (Paris: Grasset, 1987). Furthermore the apartment at 102, boulevard Haussmann in which Proust wrote his novel had previously been his uncle's, and Proust had seen his uncle die in the very room that was to become his own room. See Milton L. Miller, *Nostalgia: A Psychoanalytic Study of Marcel Proust* (Cambridge, Mass.: Riverside Press, 1956), 15.

18. Unless, of course, the house in Combray is considered as not belonging to Marcel and his family, since it is Aunt Léonie's; but if that is the case, all of "Combray" would be an example of avuncular hospitality, and the scene with Uncle Adolphe simply an extension of that form of hospitality.

19. Charlus is the most "avuncular" character in the novel, being both Saint-Loup's uncle and Madame de Villeparisis's nephew. Jupien, as we have seen, is generally identified as an uncle ("la nièce de Jupien" is a fairly important character), although he is sometimes referred to as his "niece's" father (Clarac and Ferré call this a "confusion" on Proust's part, 3.1231). Moreover let us not forget that both Charlus and Jupien play the role of ersatz father to Jupien's niece, since Charlus will later decide to adopt her (3.311)—his brother will even try to suggest that she is Charlus's (illegitimate) daughter (3.666). But as soon as Charlus has married off his adopted daughter and thus assured the transmission of his heritage, she immediately dies (3.671). It is as if his attempt to transform his identity from avuncular to paternal were being rejected by the narrative.

20. It is tempting to point out here that the French word *tante* (aunt) is a common slang expression for an effeminate male homosexual. This assimilation of effeminate males to lateral female relatives is also operative in the English "sissy."

21. An important exception being Odysseus's recognition by his dog Argos in Book 20, which happens even more quickly.

22. Book 19, lines 394, 418, 430, 437, 455, 459, and 466, each time by the phrase

"the sons of Autolykos," the sons of Odysseus's maternal grandfather being, of course, his maternal uncles.

23. Erich Auerbach, "Odysseus' Scar," in George Steiner and Robert Fagles, eds., *Homer: A Collection of Critical Essays* (Englewood Cliffs, N.J.: Prentice-Hall, 1962), 20–23.

24. Georg Lukács distinguishes between the novel and the epic by saying that while in the epic life is so imbued with meaning that temporality poses no essential problem, in the novel "meaning is separated from life, and hence the essential from the temporal." See *The Theory of the Novel*, trans. Anna Bostock (Cambridge: MIT Press, 1971), 122. To this remarkable formulation I would add that even though at every stage of Odysseus's journey one might consider meaning to be immanent to experience, the narrative also retains a forward impulse and need that can be released only through a successful homecoming. I would also argue that in Proust, although there is essentially no "homecoming," once homelessness has been revealed to be an inescapable state for the narrator, the essential is, paradoxically, no longer separable from the temporal but rather inherent to it—that is, inherent to the temporality of the narrative, itself the state of homelessness.

25. I am in slight disagreement here with Jakobson, who claims that Odysseus's deepest desire is not to come home but rather to tell stories (*Poétique de la prose*, 75). I would argue that the work's impulse to make Odysseus arrive home is as strong as its impulse to postpone his arrival indefinitely, and that the strength of the epic lies in the balancing of the two impulses.

26. Genette, *Figures III*, 56–57.

CHAPTER 2

1. Proust, *A la recherche du temps perdu*, 3.458–60.

2. Mikhaïl Bakhtin, *The Dialogic Imagination*, trans. Caryl Emerson and Michael Holquist (Austin: University of Texas Press, 1981), 5.

3. I am speaking here of the underlying strategies of intertextual readings rather than of the chronology of texts and intertexts. It is possible for a critic to establish an intertext that, unlike the New Testament in relation to the Old, *precedes* a text in time—and still to do so with a fervor similar to that of readers of the New Testament who consider that later work as an indispensable intertext to the Hebrew Bible.

4. Georges Cattaui, "L'Oeuvre de Proust, son architecture, son orchestration, sa symbolique," *Critique* 130 (March 1958): 199.

5. Marcel Muller, *Préfiguration et structure romanesque* (Lexington, Ky.: French Forum Monographs no. 14, 1979), 29, 84, and 38, respectively.

6. David J. A. Clines, *The Theme of the Pentateuch* (Sheffield, England: Journal for the Study of the Old Testament, 1978), 29.

7. Hebrew actually does not have a present tense in its verbal system; the present must be expressed by a verbal adjective that is inflected according to gender and number, like nouns and adjectives, but not according to grammatical person, like verbs.

8. Clines, *The Theme of the Pentateuch*, 25.

9. This is clear in the anecdote of Swann *père*'s idiosyncratic way of mourning the death of his wife, about whom he thinks "often, but just a little at a time" ("Souvent, mais peu à la fois," 1.15).

10. The story of Cain, the first farmer, immediately links agriculture and evil.

11. Jeanne Bem, "Le Juif et l'homosexuel dans '*A la recherche du temps perdu*': fonctionnements textuels," in *Littérature* 37 (February 1980): 104–6.

12. This is never made explicit, but as Bem points out (105), Albertine's disdain for the Simonnets (1.845; 2.368) is undoubtedly related to her hatred of Jews (2.356). I might add that the name "Simonnet" (with two ns) is quite close to "Swann," *m* being an upside-down *w*. "Simonnet" might well be related to the common Jewish name "Simon," although the latter is, appropriately, ambiguous: in the recent German film *Heimat*, the protagonists, a Christian family named Simon, frantically seek to prove that they are not Jews when the Nazis come to power.

13. Stéphane Mallarmé, *Oeuvres complètes*, ed. Henri Mondor and G. Jean-Aubry (Paris: Gallimard, Pléiade, 1945), 68. All direct quotations of Mallarmé will be taken from this edition.

14. Two other lines are also slightly misquoted in Proust's text, which gives "dans l'air" for "en l'air" and "Flamber les royaumes épars" for "Avec des royaumes épars."

15. Barbara Hardy, *The Advantage of Lyric* (Bloomington: Indiana University Press, 1977), 2.

16. A. R. Chisholm, *Towards Hérodiade: A Literary Genealogy* (Melbourne: Melbourne University Press, 1934), 138. In his biography of Mallarmé, Henri Mondor reports that a friend of Mallarmé's told him: "I admire you for the same reasons that make me admire Racine." See *Vie de Mallarmé* (Paris: Gallimard, 1941), 2.760.

17. The poem was never printed in this form during Mallarmé's lifetime, but Mondor's and Jean-Aubry's decision to publish the parts together is not arbitrary.

18. The story of Herodias seems to lend itself to the form of a triptych; another famous treatment, Flaubert's tale "Hérodias," is the last of his *Trois contes*, which are modeled after a triptych of stained-glass windows.

19. Wallace Fowlie, "Hérodiade: Myth or Heroine?" in Will L. McLendon, ed., *L'Hénaurme Siècle* (Heidelberg: Carl Winter, 1984), 170.

20. Fowlie, "Hérodiade," 173 and 172, respectively.

21. In Jean Racine, *Théâtre complet*, ed. J. Morel and A. Viala (Paris: Garnier Frères, 1980), lines 634–40. All quotations of Racine's theater will be taken from this edition, and line numbers will be bracketed in the body of the text.

22. Robert Greer Cohn comments on the parallel between Hérodiade's nurse and Oenone. *Toward the Poems of Mallarmé*, 2d ed. (Berkeley and Los Angeles: University of California Press, 1980), 54.

23. See Gardner Davies, *Mallarmé et le drame solaire* (Paris: Corti, 1959).

24. As Cohn points out in *Toward the Poems of Mallarmé*, 85.

25. See, for example, Hugo Friedrich, *The Structure of Modern Poetry*, trans. Joachim Neugroschel (Evanston: Northwestern University Press, 1974), 69–106.

26. Stéphane Mallarmé, *Poems*, trans. Roger Fry, with commentary by Charles Mauron (London: Chatto and Windus, 1936), 76.

27. Paul de Man, "Lyric and Modernity," in *Blindness and Insight: Essays in the Rhetoric of Contemporary Criticism* (Minneapolis: University of Minnesota Press, 1983), 177. Other critics, perhaps led by Albert Thibaudet's influential *La Poésie de Stéphane Mallarmé* (Paris: Gallimard, 1926), have pointed out that a number of Christian concepts underlie Mallarmé's poetic system (Thibaudet links this current of Mallarmé's work to his Platonism, 154). I am in agreement with both positions: the fact that Mallarmé's work has some Christian elements seems to me beyond debate, but the nature of those elements is evidence of a complex, often critical, and sometimes (but by no means always) irreverent relation to Christian thought.

28. This articulation is very much in keeping with one of the most remarkable features of Mallarmé's own work—the fact that he addresses enormous issues in short poems that often create an impression of miniaturization.

29. Jean Racine, *Oeuvres complètes*, ed. Raymond Picard (Paris: Gallimard, Pléiade, 1950), 1.984–85.

30. Lucien Goldmann, *Le Dieu caché* (Paris: Gallimard, 1959).

31. Of course, this movement away from tragedy does not happen once and for all in Proust's novel, but this is still a key moment. Moreover, it is perhaps not coincidental that in the climactic scene of *Le Temps retrouvé* during which Marcel's literary vocation is more fully defined, La Berma is once again alive (undoubtedly this inconsistency is due to incomplete revisions of the text) and giving a reception that Marcel declines to attend in order to go to the matinée Guermantes (3.995–99). La Berma and tragedy are thus still an alternative vocation to the novel.

32. For an extremely rich and detailed development of this intersection of texts, see Antoine Compagnon, "Proust on Racine," *Yale French Studies* 76 (1989): 21–58.

CHAPTER 3

1. For a good critical review of studies dealing with this relation, see Joyce N. Megay, *Bergson et Proust* (Paris: Vrin, 1976), especially Chapter 1, 29–50.

2. For a brief history of the revival of interest in Zeno in the past century, see Maurice Caveing, *Zénon d'Elée* (Paris: Vrin, 1982), 3–5. For a more long-range history of philosophical and mathematical reactions to Zeno across the centuries, see Jean Zafiropulo, *Vox Zenonis* (Paris: Belles-Lettres, 1958).

3. Henri Bergson, *La Pensée et le mouvant* (Geneva: Editions Albert Skira, 1946), 156. All translations from the French, unless otherwise noted, are mine.

4. Henri Bergson, *L'Evolution créatrice* (Paris: Félix Alcan, 1921), 333–34.

5. Indeed, the paradox of Achilles and the tortoise is sometimes attributed to a fellow Eleatic, Parmenides. See, for example, Yves Battistini, *Trois Présocra-*

tiques (Paris: Gallimard, 1968), 101–2. The opposing position, that of a universe in flux, was most prominently defended by Heraclitus.

6. Jean Milet, *Bergson et le calcul infinitésimal ou la raison et le temps* (Paris: Presses Universitaires de France, 1974), 53–54.

7. Bergson, *La Pensée et le mouvant*, 156.

8. Ibid., 19–20.

9. See, for example, Claudia J. Brodsky, "Remembering Swann," in *The Imposition of Form: Studies in Narrative Representation and Knowledge* (Princeton: Princeton University Press, 1987), 262–306.

10. Time in Proust has of course been treated by many critics, but I would draw particular attention to Georges Poulet, "Proust and Human Time," trans. Elliott Coleman, in René Girard, ed., *Proust: A Collection of Critical Essays* (Englewood Cliffs, N.J.: Prentice-Hall, 1962), and John Porter Houston, "Temporal Patterns in *A la recherche du temps perdu*," *French Studies* 16 (1962), 33–45.

11. Proust, *A la recherche du temps perdu*, 1.230.

12. Bergson, *La Pensée et le mouvant*, 157.

13. René Girard comments on this social organization of Proust's novel and its basis in conformity or "unité." "Les Mondes Proustiens," in *Mensonge romantique et vérité romanesque* (Paris: Grasset, 1961), esp. 197–207.

14. Gilles Deleuze, *Marcel Proust et les signes* (Paris: Presses Universitaires de France, 1964), 4.

15. Bergson, *La Pensée et le mouvant*, 145.

16. James Joyce, *Ulysses* (1914. Reprint. New York: Random House Modern Library, 1961), 783.

17. Deleuze, *Marcel Proust et les signes*, 5.

18. Albertine's response to this letter takes the form of two contradictory messages that she sends to Marcel and that he receives only after her death (3.477–78). The telegram Marcel sends to Albertine asking her to come back to him presumably does not reach her before her death, as his telegram has just been sent when he receives the telegram informing him of Albertine's death (3.476).

19. Georges Poulet, *L'Espace proustien* (Paris: Gallimard, 1963), 13.

20. Gérard Genette highlights the same sort of conflict between the general and the particular in his own critical approach to Proust. See *Narrative Discourse: An Essay in Method*, trans. Jane E. Lewin (Ithaca: Cornell University Press, 1980), 22–23.

CHAPTER 4

1. The unmitigatedly anxious and distressing mood of the film is exacerbated by Hans Werner Henze's dissonant and nerve-wracking musical score. The *petite phrase* of Vinteuil's sonata is especially inappropriate. Closer in mood to Arnold Schoenberg than to Proust's actual models (Fauré, Franck, and Saint-Saëns, among others), the little phrase in the film is also completely devoid of the gentleness, melancholy, and noble sadness that Proust's descriptions re-

peatedly attribute to the passage and that crystallize Swann's—and to some extent the narrator's—relation to temporality.

2. The single character whom this question is enough to make interesting is, appropriately, the voyeuristic Baron de Charlus, a small role that is remarkably well played by Alain Delon.

3. Schlöndorff's film may well have a number of merits on its own; it is merely as a version of Proust's work that I find it exceedingly disappointing. Perhaps it would be difficult to film "Un Amour de Swann" without dwelling on the fashions of the day to some extent, but in this film one does not manage, from beginning to end, even to push one's awareness of them into the background. A revealing commentary on the film is that it attracted the attention of at least one glossy French fashion magazine, which did a sumptuous photo layout of fashions from the film.

4. See, for example, the long description at the end of *Du côté de chez Swann* of Marcel's walks through the Bois de Boulogne as an elderly man, in *A la recherche du temps perdu*, 1.421–27. See especially 1.425–26, e.g., "How horrible!" I said to myself. "Is it possible to find these automobiles as elegant as those old carriages?" (425). Today, nearly a century after those early automobiles drove through Paris, the answer to that question—and Proust undoubtedly understood that this would be the case—is yes.

5. By Donald Spoto, Philippe Elhem, and Robin Wood, among others. Hitchcock himself thought very highly indeed of this film.

6. The Wagner opera is an important model for the film's score by Bernard Herrmann, as Donald Spoto points out in *The Art of Alfred Hitchcock* (New York: Hopkinson and Blake, 1976), 299. This is particularly interesting in that *Tristan and Isolde* plays a significant role in Proust's novel, as we shall see in Chapter 5.

7. Paris: Editions Denoël, 1958.

8. In a private communication of 3 June 1985.

9. Even when one has recognized the necessary element of subjectivity in the film, the point of view still seems to retain a detached, objective quality. As Louis Danvers puts it: "'Vertigo' seems to be the product of an external subjectivity, situated outside of the action and the screen." See "Tous les chemins mènent à 'Vertigo,'" in *Revue belge du cinéma* 9 (Autumn 1984): 15.

10. In a private communication of 30 June 1985. Taylor was uncertain whether Hitchcock himself ever read Proust, but based on his memories of Hitchcock's quite extensive personal library he thought it reasonable to assume he owned a copy of the novel, and quite possible that he read it at some point. He characterized Hitchcock as "a voracious reader once in a while."

11. In the novel the painter's name is actually spelled "Elstir," but the English pronunciation of the two names is identical.

12. For reasons of economy and simplicity, when I use the name "Madeleine" I will be referring to Judy Barton posing as Madeleine Elster, and not to Elster's real wife, unless otherwise noted.

13. This is not the reason given by Hitchcock for using the Empire Hotel on Post Street, but the name of the street nonetheless seems to comment on the

events that happen on it. See François Truffaut, *Hitchcock/Truffaut* (Paris: Ramsey, 1983), 209.

14. In fact, in the three scenes in which only (or almost only) men are present, Scottie gets nothing but ill treatment: the opening chase scene (even the policeman's attempts to help him backfire, as they compound his acrophobia with unfair guilt feelings over the policeman's death); the scene in which Elster first presents his lie to Scottie; and the inquest at which the death of the real Madeleine Elster is judged a suicide and Scottie is cruelly and unfairly reprimanded by an unfeeling judge. The world of men is thus singularly unkind to Scottie: men either dupe him or condemn him; they wrongly make him feel guilty; like the criminal in the opening scene who gets away, they make him feel like a failure. The masculine world is as strongly opposed to the world of women, first represented by the maternal Midge sketching a brassière and clucking over Scottie ("You're a big boy now . . ." "Don't be so motherly!"), as it is in the opening scenes of Proust's novel, in which the narrator's addictive "habit" is a maternal kiss, his unknown (and unwitting) enemy is Monsieur Swann, and his rather arbitrary judge is his own father.

15. ". . . one winter day, as I was arriving home, my mother, seeing how cold I was, offered me a cup of tea, which it was not my habit to drink [*contre mon habitude*]. I refused at first and then, I do not know why, changed my mind. She sent for one of those short, plump cakes called 'little madeleines.'. . ." (1.44–45).

16. There is undoubtedly a play going on here between cantilever and suspension bridges. The Golden Gate Bridge, under which Scottie saves Madeleine when she jumps into San Francisco Bay, is of course a famous suspension bridge, and might indeed be a sort of architectural reminder of Hitchcock's use of suspense. But this is far from being one of Hitchcock's most suspenseful films; in fact the reason for his rewriting *D'Entre les morts* and revealing Judy's real identity far before the end is to heighten the suspense of Scottie's discovery (*Hitchcock/Truffaut*, 206–7). Perhaps this is why the film's true emblem is not the suspension bridge but the cantilever bridge. If suspense is based upon an imminent future, then the cantilever bridge, by virtue of its context here, might well be related to Scottie's obsession with the past and his desire to transcend it; indeed for him we might even go so far as to say that once we have left him hanging in the first scene, perhaps the film's most suspenseful moment, wondering whether or not he will fall, there is not much further possibility for suspense in the rest of the film except insofar as the future is simply a discovery of the past (Judy's true identity), because Scottie has no future until he has been freed from the past. Finally, the cantilever bridge is based on a *vertical* symmetry, thereby emphasizing its association with Scottie's vertigo, his inability to transcend the past.

17. Viewing people from the back is extremely important in Hitchcock's cinema, a few prominent examples being the opening shots of *Marnie*, in which the heroine is seen only from the back; the famous scene in *Psycho* in which Mrs. Bates looks terrifyingly different from the back and from the front; and *Rear*

Window, which takes as its premise that life observed from the rear is not quite the same as it appears when seen from the front.

18. The audience gets a long, straight-on profile view of Madeleine as she approaches Scottie, but he turns toward the bar and presumably does not see it, unless perhaps he catches it in the mirror, since in a later scene the identical shot seems to be stored in his memory. When he first sees Madeleine from the front, in the flower shop, there is in fact a mirror involved, and we see Madeleine's reflection in it while Scottie sees her directly. It is as if Scottie and the audience could not both look at Madeleine directly at the same time.

19. This aspect of Midge's role is indicated by her name, "Midge Wood." Her first name suggests "Midget," which emphasizes her smallness in Scottie's eyes as opposed to Madeleine's larger-than-life status, also pointed to by the etymology of the name "Madeleine," Hebrew *migdal*, "tower" (particularly appropriate given the events of the film). Midge's last name evokes not only a civilized and slightly boring equivalent of Madeleine's fascination with sequoias, but also, more importantly, her availability ("would"); the whole story of the failed couple of Midge and Scottie, one of the film's strongest undercurrents, is summed up by this name: she "would" (have prolonged their engagement, and married him) if only he "would" (have loved her)—but he didn't, so she didn't.

20. Spoto, *The Art of Alfred Hitchcock*, 335.

21. I think this role of music is at least as important here as what Elisabeth Weis points out in her analysis: "The implication that classical music is less in touch with genuine feelings reaches its extreme with the reference to Mozart in *Vertigo*." See *The Silent Scream: Alfred Hitchcock's Sound Track* (East Brunswick, N.J.: Associated University Presses, 1982), 91.

22. I strongly disagree with those who believe that at the end of the film Scottie is about to jump off the church tower himself. I see the film's final shot, with Scottie standing and looking down from the church tower, as a demonstration that this final trauma has cured his vertigo—as Midge, in the film's second scene, reports her doctor as saying might in fact happen.

23. "So in this way, for a long time, when I was awake at night remembering Combray, all I ever saw of it was a kind of brilliant section of wall . . . ; as if Combray had been composed only of two stories linked by a thin stairway . . ." (1.43–44).

24. "What one takes in the presence of the loved one is only a negative [*cliché négatif*], one develops it later. . . ." (1.872).

25. "True life, life at last discovered and enlightened, . . . is literature. . . . But [most people] do not see it. . . . And thus their past is loaded down with countless negatives [*clichés*] that remain useless because intelligence has not 'developed' them" (3.895).

26. "Proust and Human Time," trans. Elliott Coleman, in Girard, ed., *Proust: A Collection of Critical Essays*, 175.

27. I am speaking of cinema in a purely theoretical way, as a unique medium for the representation of movement, rather than in any of its actual historical developments. Certainly cinema has techniques for portraying simultaneity,

but I think it is fair to say that it is not this capacity, but rather that of representing movement, that specifically differentiates it as cinema.

28. Ramon Fernandez, "In Search of the Self," in Girard, ed., *Proust: A Collection of Critical Essays*, 143–44, emphasis in the original. Fernandez explicitly mentions Bergson in this context (144, n. 8) and suggests that Proust is at some times a Bergsonian, at others an anti-Bergsonian.

29. Georges Poulet, *L'Espace proustien* (Paris: Gallimard, 1963), 39–40.

CHAPTER 5

1. Georges Piroué, *Proust et la musique du devenir*. Part 4: "La structure musicale d'*A la recherche du temps perdu*" (Paris: Editions Denoël, 1960), 167–280. A recent study on Proust's interest in music is Jean-Jacques Nattiez, *Proust as Musician*, trans. Derrick Puffett (Cambridge: Cambridge University Press, 1989).

2. Emile Bedriomo, *Proust, Wagner, et la coïncidence des arts*. Etudes littéraires françaises no. 34 (Tubingen: Gunter Narr, 1984).

3. Proust, *A la recherche du temps perdu*, 1.64.

4. Particularly by Françoise (e.g., 1.108), by the curé (e.g., 1.104), and by Eulalie (e.g., 1.106).

5. E.g., "My grandfather, . . . whose pronouncements . . . often allowed me later on to absolve faults that I would have been inclined to condemn" (1.15). In fact the grandfather, as we shall see in greater detail in Chapter 6, is generally presented as the opposite of his wife; he is a *bon vivant* with a wicked sense of humor and little moral fiber. His favorite line of Corneille, for example, appears to be "Lord, how many virtues you make me detest!" ("La Mort de Pompée," 3.4); he slightly misquotes the line with great relish (1.27).

6. Marcel Proust, *Jean Santeuil*, ed. Pierre Clarac (Paris: Gallimard, Pléiade, 1971), 203.

7. Marcel Proust, *Essais et articles, Contre Sainte-Beuve*, ed. Pierre Clarac and Yves Sandre (Paris: Gallimard, Pléiade, 1971), 382.

8. Proust, *Jean Santeuil*, 224.

9. In fact we have no way of knowing whether the grandmother actually takes the elevator to go up to the rooms on this particular occasion, since Marcel goes up before she does and we are simply told that "my grandmother came in" (1.667), but we may assume that her fondness for physical exercise—apparent from her walks in all kinds of inclement weather (e.g., 1.102) and her delight at going out to open the door for Swann as "a pretext to take yet another stroll around the garden" (1.14)—extends to vertical walks. The fact that Marcel does not even seem to have the strength to push the button to call for the elevator himself (1.665) harkens back to the doorknob of his bedroom in Combray ("Ce *bouton* de la porte de ma chambre") which "seemed to open all by itself, without my needing to turn it" (1.10).

10. This is particularly clear in Balbec, when the grandmother seems to be neglecting Marcel but is in fact trying to hide her illness (1.787), and also in the

incident of the photograph she has taken so that he might have it after her death, a fact that he discovers only much later (2.776–78).

11. These are of course far from being the only important musical figures in either Proust's novel or his life. Another obvious contrast in the novel is between the monumental music of Wagner and the ephemeral Debussy (e.g., 2.812–15). In fact this sort of polarity organized around two artists can be found quite frequently in the novel.

12. *Album Proust*, ed. Pierre Clarac and André Ferré (Paris: Gallimard, Pléiade 1965), 90 (for the reference to Mozart) and 122 (for the reference to Wagner). In his biography of Proust, George D. Painter expresses the opinion that this evolution from Mozart to Wagner is in some sense an inevitable one in Proust: "Proust was by nature a Wagnerian." In *Marcel Proust, A Biography* (New York: Vintage, 1959), 1.52. In addition to the explicit pairings of Mozart and Wagner already mentioned, a page of *Jean Santeuil* juxtaposes a comment about Mozart and one about *Tristan and Isolde*: the rather ridiculous Baron de Berlinges, a precursor of Cottard, is equally mystified by "a particular incident in the life of Mozart" and a joke about *Tristan and Isolde* (*Jean Santeuil*, 716); is this not once again an indication that in Proust's mind the two composers are somehow linked?

13. Indeed, with regard to Mozart's comparatively restrained style, I might mention an anecdote that, given the grandmother's association with Mozart and the novel's description of her emotional death scene, may not be gratuitous. On his deathbed Mozart himself was working on his uncompleted *Requiem*, and as *la petite histoire*—or at least the end of the autograph of the *Requiem*—would have it, the final phrase he wrote was a very long ascending scale of tremendous emotional impact (the opening bars of the *Lacrimosa dies illa*).

14. This is particularly clear if one compares Proust's mature style with certain passages from *Contre Sainte-Beuve*, for example. Although it is difficult to generalize about such things, it would probably be safe to say that Proust moved on the whole toward a less effusive and a more restrained style as he matured.

15. Victor Zuckerkandl, *Sound and Symbol: Music and the External World* (New York: Pantheon, 1956), 35.

16. Zuckerkandl, *Sound and Symbol*, 36–37.

17. Proust attended performances of Wagner's *Tristan and Isolde* at least twice. In 1902 he saw the opera with his friends Bibesco and Fénelon. See *Marcel Proust, Selected Letters 1880–1903*, ed. Philip Kolb, with introduction by J. M. Cocking (Garden City, N.Y.: Doubleday, 1983), 239. And in 1908 he heard *Tristan* with the Duc de Guiche. See Painter, *Marcel Proust*, 2.169.

18. Raymond Mander and Joe Mitchenson, *The Wagner Companion* (London: W. H. Allen, 1977), 171.

19. Thomas Mann, "Sufferings and Greatness of Richard Wagner," in *Essays of Three Decades*, trans. H. T. Lowe-Porter (New York: Alfred A. Knopf, 1947), 351.

20. There is of course a huge literature on the Tristan Chord; a good quick

survey can be found in Serge Gut, "Encore et toujours: 'L'accord de Tristan,'" in *L'Avant-Scène* 34–35 (July–August 1981): 148–51. The Tristan Chord has also been interpreted as a forerunner of the twelve-tone system; for a good survey of the literature on this, see Martin Vogel, *Der Tristan-Akkord und die Krise der modernen Harmonie-Lehre* (Düsseldorf: Orpheus, 1962), 13–14.

21. The dominant seventh of A minor would be E–G♯–B–D; some musicologists take the liberty of reading the F in the Tristan chord as an E♯.

22. Zuckerkandl, *Sound and Symbol*, 50.

23. We do in fact get an A, an eighth-note in the same measure as the Tristan chord, but it is part of a gradual climb from G♯ to B (G♯–A–A♯–B) and creates no feeling of stability or resolution.

24. Zuckerkandl, *Sound and Symbol*, 51.

25. This famous description is anticipated by the passage in *A l'ombre des jeunes filles en fleurs* in which the G of Gilberte's signature already looks like an A (1.502).

26. For an analogous discussion, which finds anagrams of the names of Tristan and other Wagnerian heroes in a number of words used recurrently by Proust, see Jean Milly, *La Phrase de Proust* (Paris: Larousse, 1975), 67–73.

27. This is the passage that ends the recently published deathbed manuscript of *Albertine disparue*, ed. Nathalie Mauriac and Etienne Wolff (Paris: Grasset, 1987), 158. It is thus one of the very last sections of the novel on which Proust worked, and although he changed nothing in the description of the A and the G, the fact that he decided to end *Albertine disparue* here certainly underscores the importance of this passage.

28. This pronunciation, although it is the opposite of linguistic "syncope"— the elision of one or more syllables in the middle of a word—does create a feeling of musical syncopation, an upsetting of the word's normal rhythm.

29. This articulation is almost explicit, since the grandmother falls ill on the Champs-Elysées, in the very place where Marcel and Gilberte have their amorous wrestling match (1.493–94), and immediately after the narrative of the grandmother's death comes that of Albertine's visit to Marcel in Paris (2.358–70), which more or less begins their physical relationship.

30. If we recall that the grandmother's death is explicitly compared to Isolde's love-death, her syncopes may not be completely unrelated to the syncopation in the section of the love-death immediately preceding the climax of *Tristan and Isolde*. Elliott Zuckerman calls this syncopation virtually the only "rhythmic device worth mentioning" in the entire opera. See *The First Hundred Years of Wagner's Tristan* (New York: Columbia University Press, 1962), 18.

31. Paul de Man has eloquently shown the limitations of the formula "plus tard, j'ai compris," which "punctuates the entire novel like an incantation." In *Allegories of Reading* (New Haven: Yale University Press, 1979), 78.

CHAPTER 6

1. J. E. Rivers, *Proust and the Art of Love* (New York: Columbia University Press, 1980), 10.

2. Milton L. Miller, *Nostalgia: A Psychoanalytic Study of Marcel Proust* (Cambridge, Mass.: Riverside Press, 1956), 2–3.

3. Ibid., 9–10.

4. Randolph Splitter, *Proust's Recherche: A Psychoanalytic Interpretation* (Boston: Routledge and Kegan Paul, 1981), 43–44.

5. I do not actually believe these two images of the grandmother to be contradictory (although they could be and remain equally valid). In Chapter 5 I emphasized the grandmother's strength of self-resistance, whereas here I will describe her as a melancholic whose central characteristic is self-criticism (and veiled criticism of others). These two readings could be integrated into a single conception of a woman who draws a certain strength of character from her dissatisfaction with herself and with others, a person whose overdeveloped critical agency accompanies—and even to some extent contributes to—a tremendous strength of will.

6. See *The Standard Edition of the Complete Psychological Works of Sigmund Freud*, trans. and ed. James Strachey (1957. Reprint. London: Hogarth Press, 1968), 14.240–41. All quotations of Freud are from this edition, and references will be given in the body of the text. Unless otherwise noted, all references are to Volume 14 of this edition.

7. There is a discussion of a similar phenomenon in paranoids in "On Narcissism: An Introduction."

8. "The ego ideal had the task of repressing the Oedipus complex; indeed, it is to that revolutionary event that it owes its existence." See "The Ego and the Id" (1923).

9. "Editor's Note," in "Mourning and Melancholia."

10. Proust, *A la recherche du temps perdu*, 1.11–12.

11. See Chapter 5 for a more detailed discussion of this point.

12. Randolph Splitter oversimplifies the mother's character when he claims that she "proves most faithful, it seems, not to her husband but to another woman, her own mother, Marcel's grandmother. . . ." (*Proust's Recherche*, 45). This may well be true in the absolute, but it neglects the much subtler suggestions of the mother's (perhaps undeserved) attachment to her husband. See, for example, the loving but slightly distant look she gives him so as not to "penetrate the mystery of his superior qualities" (1.11).

INDEX

chapter one

My cousin Nick stomped over to our table. "I don't believe it. My lunch is gone again!" He scowled and sat down. "This is the second time this week."

"You probably just forgot it at home," Robyn suggested.

"No chance. I never forget my lunch," Nick said.

I could relate. By noon I was so hungry, I was ready to eat the linoleum in the school hallway. I never forget my lunch either.

"Hey, Nick! You finished unpacking, yet?" I had to shout to make myself heard over the clanging of metal chairs and the loud voices. Lunch hour in our school was like the monkey house at the zoo. And it didn't smell much better at the moment, either. "Robyn, if you're gonna bring roadkill sandwiches, you have to sit somewhere else."

Robyn flicked her ponytail over her shoulder and took another bite. "It's not roadkill," she answered. "It's liverwurst and onion."

"Augh! Same thing!" I made a face.

Nick grinned hungrily. "At this point, anything looks good." He stared at Robyn's sandwich. Robyn sighed and handed him half.

"Nick, no!" I clutched my hair with both hands. "It's suicide! I'll give you some of mine!"

"I'll take all offers," Nick said with his mouth full. "I'm starving." He took another bite. "And no, we're not finished unpacking. At least Dad found the boxes with my clothes in them last night. Now I can finally change my socks."

Nick had just moved to Calgary a few weeks ago with my aunt and uncle, and was new at my school.

I rummaged in my backpack for my lunch. It seemed kind of empty. I peered inside, then shook it. A bag of carrots fell out. That was all. "Did anyone see my lunch? I brought a ham-and-cheese sub."

Robyn and Nick shook their heads. "Maybe you left it in your locker," Nick said.

"No way. I know I had it," I said. I opened my bag of carrots in disgust and looked at Robyn suspiciously. "If you swiped my lunch because I said your sandwiches smell like roadkill, it's not funny. I could starve to death."

"I never took anything, I swear," Robyn said. She reached into her lunch bag, and a puzzled look crossed her face. "I don't believe it! I brought extra chocolate bars to share with you doofs, but they're missing."

"What!" My stomach rumbled with disappointment. My only lifeline until four o'clock was slipping away. "How can they be gone?"

"You probably ate them already," Nick said.

Robyn shot him a sour look. "I think I'd know if I ate three chocolate bars."

The three of us stared at each other.

"Something very weird is going on," Robyn said.

"Heads up!" someone yelled. Before any of us could move, something hit Robyn in the head. Pink goo splattered everywhere and slimy red things dripped down her hair.

Robyn shrieked. "What *is* this!" she yelled, flicking a red glob onto the table.

I leaned closer and sniffed. "Yogurt," I pronounced. "Strawberry, I think."

"Yogurt!" Robyn turned around and her gaze landed on Cray Simmons, who was at the table directly behind us.

Cray is one of those kids who enjoys stirring up trouble. Me, Robyn and some other kids used to play football with him after lunch, but his mouthy, super-jock attitude really bugged Robyn, so she quit.

He hasn't stopped baiting her since.

Cray's mouth twitched, and I could tell he was trying not to laugh—Robyn was so obviously furious. She *did* look pretty funny.

"Cray! You butt head! I'll get you for that!" Robyn hollered.

"I didn't do it," he said. "Why would I waste my yogurt on you, rich girl?"

"You're such a jerk." Robyn whipped the remains of her sandwich at Cray. His smirk changed to astonishment as bits of liverwurst clung to his shirt.

"Hey!" he said, looking angry. "What the—!"

That's as far as he got.

"Food fight!" someone yelled. Within seconds, the air was thick with flying potato chips, cheezies and other odds and ends. Someone shook a pop and opened it. Wet foam sprayed everywhere. Cray stood paralyzed as bubbling drops trickled down his forehead. A tomato slice hit Nick on the cheek and stuck until he shook it off.

"Ow!" he yelled. He reached for Robyn's

half-empty juice box and prepared to throw it into the fray.

"Stop!" Cray shouted suddenly, recovering movement at last. "Quit being so stupid!" He dove over his table and grabbed Nick's wrist, forcing him to drop the juice box.

Nick shoved him away. "You started it!" He took the remnants of Robyn's sandwich and squished it into Cray's face.

"I did not, butt face!" Cray gasped through the liverwurst. Cray twisted away, a crust of bread dangling from one ear. He tackled Nick. The two of them went down hard and began wrestling under the table. Nick's skinny arms were no match for Cray, and Cray soon grabbed him in a headlock.

"All right! That's enough!" the principal bellowed. Ms. Beaudry marched into the room, and quiet instantly fell, except for the scuffling under our table, where Nick and Cray were still locked in battle.

"Crawley Simmons! Get up, now!" Ms. Beaudry's face was bright red. I could almost see the steam coming from her ears. Cray, who hates being called by his full name,